"Stewart helps people b ....ize *their undiscovered capa* .... 'or *everyone is to understa* .... *i's circumstance. Stewart* ......ana and apply *mind-tools; his hyperspace education opens your eyes to find the truth in relation to man, mind, and cosmos."*
Maarten P., The Netherlands

"Stewart's work has helped me expand my mind to new horizons; layers and layers of what were previously unthinkable; ways of being that were unimaginable have become my reality. His techniques have helped me take back my power in life. What I previously gave up on are now open doors to the next level/phase. What I always felt was out there, and searched and searched for, Stewart knows and taught me to know, too. How can you not love Stewart?"
Joe P., California

"I have studied Stewart's work for several years. I know from personal experience that Stewart's information is reliable. Whenever I apply his techniques I find them to be right. Janet's work offers a wide range of tools on how to 'know by knowing' which makes it possible for everyone to become his/her own authority in life, as well as achieve optimal vertical growth."
Claus S., Germany

"Stewart and Janet cut to the heart of the issues with total candor. Their insight, wisdom, and clarity, laced with a fair amount of humor, have been essential to my daunting task of self-discovery."
Cindy H., Texas

"Janet's techniques have taught me how to access information and communicate with a part of myself that has the answers and experiences to finally do what I came here to do. I have learned that the passions I have had for so long, that I thought unimportant and just passing thoughts, turned out to worthwhile clues to the hidden gifts I have always had. I did not realize this until Janet accessed what she did from my Oversoul and what is better, is that I am now learning to do this myself."
Diana H., Alaska

THE
HYPERSPACE
HELPER
A USER-FRIENDLY GUIDE

**By Stewart A. Swerdlow
and Janet D. Swerdlow**

Expansions Publishing Company, Inc.
P.O. Box 12, St. Joseph MI 49085 U.S.A.

The Hyperspace Helper: A User-Friendly Guide
Copyright © 2004 Expansions Publishing Company, Inc.

Cover, Typography, and Book Layout by L'OR Intuitives
Editor: Janet Swerdlow
Published by: Expansions Publishing Company, Inc.
                       P.O. Box 12
                       Saint Joseph MI 49085 U.S.A.
                       269-429-8615

                       0-9740144-1-9

For further information contact Expansions Publishing Company, Inc.
P.O. Box 12, Saint Joseph MI 49085 U.S.A.
email: stewart@stewartswerdlow.com
       janet@janetswerdlow.com
Website address: www.stewartswerdlow.com

DEDICATION

To Lori Sarich, Graphic Artist and friend, and Kim Mazzola, Webmaster and friend. These women are instrumental to our work and dedicated beyond the call of duty. We are forever grateful to them for their superb work and unending support. Because of them, our books are possible.

Contents

T~Bar Balancing

Every human being has an archetype that emanates from the pineal gland that projects into his/her personal energetic web, or "aura." This archetype, called a "T-Bar" is a function of genetics, working to balance the left and right hemispheres of the brain so that thinking does not go to extremes. The pineal gland also connects to the pituitary, thyroid, thymus, and hypothalamus glands to regulate and balance the chemical and hormonal flows of the body. The pineal gland is located at the very center of the head at the base of where the left and right hemispheres meet. The pineal gland is not at the forehead as most people believe, although there are nerve-ending connections from it to the forehead.

In human beings there are three basic shapes to the T-Bar archetype, depending upon your genetics. This archetype can look like an upper case "T", a cross, or an ankh. All three T-Bar archetypes are equal in value; one is not better than another.
As a general recommendation, you should balance your T-Bar archetype in the morning before getting out of bed and in the evening before going to sleep. Also balance it before any visualization or meditation, and anytime that you feel unbalanced

or unsettled. Use the following method:

Center your consciousness at the pineal gland in royal blue.

*Within two or three seconds, you should see your
T-Bar shape.*

*Depending upon your emotions or thoughts at that moment,
you might see the crossbars leaning, tilting or twisting in
some way. However, no matter how you see it, mentally
straighten out the crossbars so that they are completely
perpendicular to one another, forming right angles.*

*You can then press an imaginary set button underneath the
T-Bar to maintain the balance.*

If you cannot see your T-Bar archetype for whatever reason, then instead at the pineal gland you can create a royal blue circle with a royal blue dot in the center. The act of centering the dot in the circle is equal to balancing the arms of the T-Bar archetype. You can use either method interchangeably.

If necessary, you can draw a T-Bar archetype or circle with dot on a piece of paper, or even make one that you can look at, as visual aids.

Simple Breathing Exercise

Breathing properly is obviously very important for people. Over the millennia, the atmosphere on the Earth has changed drastically. The contents of the gasses in the air have been altered. In modern times, the human alveoli, or air sacs, of the lungs can only hold .065 carbon dioxide. This is because at night the green plants take in oxygen and release carbon dioxide. The process is then reversed during the day.

In ancient times when there were many more green plants on the surface of the Earth, much more carbon dioxide was released at night. Humans in those days were then able to absorb more carbon dioxide in their lungs to survive the night. Our species has adapted to this change in the carbon dioxide levels so that we can no longer inhale so much of this gas.

For this reason, it is imperative to always inhale through the nostrils and exhale through the mouth. There are filters in the sinus cavities that clean the inhaled air so that this air can be exchanged in the lungs. When you breathe out, exhale through the mouth so that there is nothing blocking the contaminated air. If you breathe out through the nostrils, you will contaminate the inner side of the air filters without any way of cleaning them. This is what causes infections and other illnesses. The outer side of the filter, facing toward the nostrils, is easily cleaned via sneezing or blowing your nose.

The following is a good method of breathing for energy and oxygenation:

Slowly inhale through the nostrils deeply into the lungs and hold for a few seconds.

Visualize contaminates and toxins exiting the lungs.

Blow out slowly through the mouth.

Visualize a medium green color filling up the lungs as you inhale. This represents the color of oxygen. Then, blow out through the mouth any other colors that do not belong in the lungs.

It is best to do this for about two minutes in the morning and another minute in the late afternoon or evening. This will oxygenate and energize you. It is also a good idea to take two or three of these breaths before any visualization or meditation.

Chakra Spinning

Every living human being has a chakra system. The word "chakra" is a Hindu/ Sanskrit word that means "wheel," referring to the way chakras spin within the energy system of the physical body.

Humans have seven main chakra centers, located from the perineum up to the crown. Each one has a specific function, color, and meaning, and corresponds to specific organs located in that part of the body.

The human chakra system is as follows:

Grounding Center
Actually, this is not a chakra at all, but rather the Earth's magnetic field connecting to the body. This extends from the feet to the perineum. The color here is brown.

Root Chakra
This is located at the perineum and extends to the top of the pubic bone. The color here is pale red.

Sacral Chakra

This chakra is located between the top of the pubic bone and the navel. The color here is pale orange.

Solar Plexus Chakra

This chakra is located between the navel and the sternum. The color here is pale yellow.

Heart Chakra

This chakra is situated between the sternum and the clavicle bone. The color here is medium green.

Throat Chakra

This chakra starts at the base of the throat and extends to just below the tip of the nose. The color here is ice blue.

Pineal Chakra

This chakra is located from the tip of the nose to the middle of the forehead. The color here is royal blue.

Crown Chakra

This chakra is located at the top of the skull. The color here is violet.

It is absolutely necessary for every human being to begin the day by spinning their chakras. Do it before getting out of bed in the morning. You may either spin them in a clockwise or counterclockwise motion, whichever one is better for you. Please note, however, that all chakras must be spun in the same direction each day. The only time it is advisable to reverse the spinning direction is to counter the effects of a traumatic or particularly stressful day. Do this by spinning from the top down.

When spinning your chakras, begin by visualizing yourself in a cylindrical tube with each of the specific colors in their respective locations. Next, visualize brown in the Grounding

Center. Work your way up to the crown using the appropriate color in each chakra band. Remember to always spin all chakra bands in the same direction.

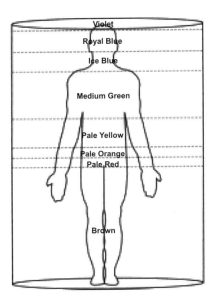

Ultimate Protection Technique

The *Ultimate Protection Technique* is a visualization designed to protect whatever you place inside of it. This technique is a geometric shape that is, according to Bible Code studies, the master shape of the God-Mind. All other shapes, archetypes, and letters can be found within it.

Visualize yourself, or whatever you wish to protect, inside a violet tetrahedron. Then, place this shape inside a violet octahedron. You may also place a gold ring around this geometric shape.

The *Ultimate Protection Technique* is so powerful that it will last three or four days without having to re-create it.

The Golden Altar

The *Golden Altar* is sometimes also called the *Forgiving and Releasing Altar*. This exercise is designed to release the images from the mind-pattern which perpetuate negative cycles that occur in your life, such as isolation, abandonment, and low self-worth issues. These mind-patterns are formulated and imprinted by early life interpersonal experiences as well as in simultaneous existences. Follow the preliminaries before beginning.

The Golden Altar Visualization Preliminaries

Take two or three cleansing breaths.

Center your consciousness in royal blue at the pineal gland.

Balance your T-Bar archetype, or center the dot in the circle at your pineal gland, all in royal blue.

Put the rest of your body in gold. Use a visual aid if necessary.

The Golden Altar Visualization

Visualize a golden altar in front of you. The altar can look like anything you need an altar to look like. On the altar, place a person that you need to forgive and release. Most people find it beneficial to start with a parent.

Using a golden frequency line, connect your heart chakra to the heart chakra of this person. Now, the two of you are connected heart-to-heart by a golden line.

Mentally say the following to this person:

I forgive you and release you from all negative experiences between us, now and in the past, whether real or imagined. I forgive you and release you.

As you say the last line, visualize the person fading off of the altar in a flash of violet.

When you are done with the above, you can put the next person on the altar and repeat the exercise. You can do this with as many people in one session as you feel comfortable. However, no matter how many people you do in one session, always forgive and release yourself last by saying the following:

I forgive and release myself from all negative experiences that I have attracted to myself in this lifetime now and in the past, whether real or imagined. I forgive and release myself.

Fade yourself off the altar, immediately putting yourself in a brown color. The color brown acts as a safety net that pulls you back to the present moment safely, grounding and balancing you.

You will probably need to do this exercise quite a number of times with the same people. This may take a few weeks, a few months, and perhaps with some people, this may take a year or more. However, one day you will go to do the exercise and you will not be able to see the person on the altar any more. He/she simply will not materialize. When this happens, you will know that the image is finally released from the mind-pattern. Then, everyone who is in your life right now who reflected that mind-pattern for you will either change the way they deal with you, or they will not be in your life anymore.

This is a positive experience because when someone loves you unconditionally, he/she accepts you regardless of your mind-pattern. However, when someone is in your life merely to reflect a negative image that you project, then that person can no longer be in your life once you stop projecting the image. So, over the weeks and months that you do this work, you will see some people fading out of your life while new people enter your life. These new people will be unconditionally accepting of you and more permanent.

Using the *Golden Altar* visualization is like physical exercise. The more you do it, the better the results. Be consistent and persistent. This exercise works 100% of the time, but remember that you are the only one who can do it for yourself.

Green Spiral Staircase

The *Green Spiral Staircase* visualization is an investigative procedure designed to mentally time-travel to specific events in your existence that are blocked from reaching your conscious mind. Use of this visualization allows you to identify specific individuals who are responsible for influencing and imprinting created mind-patterns within you. Once these memories surface to allow identification of these individuals, you can then use the *Golden Altar* visualization to completely release the mind-pattern.

The Green Spiral Staircase Visualization Preliminaries

Take two or three cleansing breaths.

Center your consciousness in royal blue at the pineal gland.

Balance your T-Bar archetype, or center the dot in the circle at your pineal gland, all in royal blue.

Put the rest of your body in medium green to activate the memory centers of the brain. Use a visual aid if necessary.

The Green Spiral Staircase Visualization

Visualize a green spiral staircase in front of you in the same medium green in which your body is now.

Focus on a specific event, time period, or place that you need to remember in detail.

Start descending the staircase while holding this thought in mind.

At some point, you will feel a need or urge to step off of the staircase. This signifies that you have reached the layer in your subconscious mind that holds the memory.

Step off the staircase.

Observe whatever scenes are in front of you as if they were on a television set on in a movie.
<u>Do not</u> participate in them.

If you become upset or traumatized to the point that you no longer wish to continue, immediately place yourself completely in brown. Discontinue the exercise.

If you see a scene and wonder if it is true, a product of your imagination, or even a hallucination, place the scene in pale orange. Pale orange is the color of absolute truth. A true scene stays in pale orange. If not, you will see the color change.

Continue to observe the scenes in front of you for as long as you wish.

When you have seen enough, or if the scene ends, go back up the staircase to the place where you began and stop.

Do not go beyond this place.
Step off the staircase.

Place yourself in brown.

Balance your T-Bar archetype.

Write down your observations.

Most likely, you will probably need to do this exercise several times to bring the memory you are exploring to the surface. Your mind will show you only the pertinent information that you currently need to know, rather than give you a minute-by-minute description.

Be patient and do not give up. Some people report blockages when they step off the staircase and cannot see anything, even though they know that something is there. If this happens, be creative. Mentally devise methods that allow you to break through the memory barriers. For example, you might create a violet sledgehammer to break through any walls in front of you, or a spotlight to illuminate any hidden or dark scenes. This is your own mind. You can invent anything you need at any moment to improve your visualization work.

Being consistent and persistent are both extremely important. Stay within the context of the current lifetime because resolving issues here resolves the same issues in other timelines. Work with what is in front of you at the moment. Remember to do the *Golden Altar* visualization with the individual you identify using the *Green Spiral Staircase* visualization.

The Child Within

There is a child within each person who has not developed into an adult. This little person causes you to emotionally react to difficult or unhappy interpersonal situations in your life. Close, personal relationships are especially vulnerable to instantly bringing out emotional reactions from the little child within. The results can be disastrous for all involved.

The following visualization is designed to mature this child so that he/she reacts as an adult rather than as a child.

The Child Within Visualization Preliminaries

Take two or three cleansing breaths.

Center your consciousness in royal blue at the pineal gland.

Balance your T-Bar archetype, or center the dot in the circle at your pineal gland,all in royal blue.

The Child Within Visualization

Move the center of consciousness slowly down from the pineal gland to the center of the heart chakra. Do this by climbing down a ladder, descending in an elevator, or simply move the center of awareness from the pineal to heart area.

Once you reach the heart chakra, place yourself in medium green.

See a door in front of you. Observe whether it is open or closed, locked or unlocked. Observe the type of door as well as its handle. All details are symbolic of your mind-pattern and emotional status.

Open the door, regardless of how it looks. Observe what is inside.

Now, walk through the door into your heart chakra, observing everything that you see.

Eventually, you see a small child coming toward you. Observe his/her age, as this is when your emotional development was arrested. Observe the child's clothing, face, gender, etc.

Ask the child his/her name. Introduce yourself. Pick up the child. Hold him/her close to your heart. Tell him/her that everything is all right, and that you will protect him/her.

Observe all changes, within you and in the scene around you.

Walk back to the door through which you entered.

As you exit, leave the door open.

Slowly move your consciousness back to the pineal gland using the same method that you used to descend.

Place yourself in royal blue when you reach the pineal gland.

Balance your T-Bar archetype, or center the dot in the circle.

Take a cleansing breath.

Now place yourself in brown.

Write down your observations so that you can interpret them to better understand your emotional structure.

You have now grown up the small child within. Observe your interpersonal reactions with others to see how you have changed.

Grounding & Balancing

Grounding and balancing are associated with the color, brown. Energetically the Earth's gravitational field is brown. This why dirt, sand, tree bark, small insects, and animals are all in a brown tone, because they all resonate with the Earth's gravitational field.

Human legs and feet, which are not part of the chakra system, also resonate to the brown gravitational fields of the Earth.

Whenever you feel upset, unsettled, emotionally disturbed, or agitated for whatever reason, balance your T-Bar archetype or center the royal blue dot in the circle at your pineal gland. Then, place yourself completely in brown, both in and around the body. This makes you feel grounded and balanced. The negative sensations will stop and you will be able to handle what is in front of you.

Because brown has to do with grounding, never use this color while flying in an airplane or riding in an elevator for obvious reasons. Refer to the protection techniques elsewhere in this book.

Spending time in a natural environment like a beach, forest, or park also helps to ground and balance. Gardening and caring for house plants adds balancing and grounding energy.

Smoking cigarettes puts brown in the auric field. This is why when some people feel nervous they get the urge to smoke. Using brown in and through you diminishes, and can even negate, the urge to smoke. Try this if you are a smoker.

Eating brown or heavy foods is another grounding technique. This is why eating chocolate or meat is common for people who are nervous or upset.

Use any visual aid necessary to see the brown. You can wrap yourself in a brown towel or robe, or wear brown clothing. The shade is simply a matter of intensity—the deeper the brown color, the deeper the grounding and the longer it lasts. Decorate your home and/or workplace with brown to help keep you centered.

Brown also represents the present moment. Using brown helps you to stay focused in the present moment and aids in concentration. So, go to brown and go to town!

General Health & Wellbeing

The following information is very basic and general health and wellbeing suggestions to improve your daily life. For those of you who are interested in more detailed work, read my *Healer's Handbook*, or watch my *Triad Healing Seminar* on DVD.

Vitamins & Supplements

Each person needs a daily multiple vitamin geared for his/her gender. These days, foods are so depleted and genetically altered that regardless of what or how you eat, it is no longer possible to get the proper amount of nutrients from the food you ingest. For this reason I suggest the following supplements on a daily basis:

Immune System
1000 mg of Vitamin C
Odorless garlic
Eat onions and greens

Nervous System/Hair/Skin
1000 mg Omega 3 Fish Oils
or two tablespoons high quality cod liver oil
Horsetail herb
Jojoba shampoo
Apply castor oil on the skin at night

Digestion
Fresh pineapple and/or papaya
Fresh lime and/or lemon juice
Ginger or chamomile tea
Live culture yogurt and/or acidophilus capsules

Muscles
Red meat, fish, turkey, chicken
Vanadium
Nuts
Whey

Building Blood
Black bread
Red wine
Purple grape juice
Red meat
Greens

Brain
Inositol with choline
Olive oil
Gingko biloba

Immune System
Hyssop
Immuplex by Standard Process
Sea salt, sprinkled on food or in your bath
Echinacea (for less than 3 weeks at a time)
Garlic

Water

All humans and animals should drink only distilled water. This is most natural to the human body. The quantity for each individual depends on your personal physical body. Over-hydration is more dangerous than dehydration. Too much water causes the cells to fill with fluid, preventing nutrients and oxygen from passing through. Over-hydration can also cause the brain to swell and the digestive system to fail.

The larger the person, the more water needed; the smaller the person, the less water needed. Weather and work conditions are also a factor. Study your own body to understand its specific needs.

Exercise

Everyone should exercise. The amount and type depends upon your individual needs. Generally, each person should do 60% weight-training and 40% aerobics weekly. You need to move. Do not be sedentary. Every person can do *something*, even if it is just walking around a room, or swinging your arms.

Extremely thin and wiry people should not be doing aerobics. Extremely overweight people should not be lifting heavy weights. Know yourself and your current physical boundaries. Change your boundaries slowly and gradually. Exercise with someone experienced, or with professional training, if possible.

Food

Not everyone needs to eat three full meals every day. Some people need to eat five meals per day plus snacks. Others only need to eat very little every day. Do not put yourself in a set classification. Humans are designed to eat on demand—not by a clock or societal rules.

When you crave a particular food, there is a reason. There is something in that food that you need. So, eat it. Do not eat to make yourself happy or to comfort yourself—there are other things that you need to be doing for this. Eat only when you are truly hungry. Eating what you like will aid in the food's proper digestion.

Eat a full range of vegetables and fruits during the week. You do not need to eat everything in one day. Eat animal proteins of all sorts. Your body, and especially your brain, requires fat to survive, so include at least two tablespoons of good fat in your diet every day.

Eat a wide variety and styles. Try new foods and cuisines. Go for the exotic from time to time. The more interesting the food, the more interesting your life, and the more interesting you become.

Enjoy what you eat, keeping in mind that whatever you ingest is a reflection of who you are at the moment.

Sleep

Most humans need seven to eight hours of sleep every day. Sleep helps the body and mind to reset, as well as connects you more efficiently to your Oversoul and God-Mind. Everyone needs to sleep. However, not everyone needs the same amount.

As the body gets older, it requires less sleep. As your body becomes more efficient, it needs less rest. Know your own body. If there are days when it is tired, sleep more. If there are days when it is really energized, stay up longer. Allow some flexibility in your schedule.

Dreaming is a way for you to assimilate experiences and make plans. Dreams help you to understand yourself and your relationship to the God-Mind and other beings. Everyone needs to sleep.

Weight Loss

Diets do not work. Losing weight is all about the mind-patterns that you hold. Fear and insecurity, for example, cause you to insulate and gain weight. The only solution for permanent weight loss is to do release work, and deprogramming if this pertains to you.

There are foods that can support the body as you change your mind-pattern. Some assist you in losing extra fluids from the body and help to keep them away. If you eat grapefruit, apples, low-fat meats, hot spices, and wild rice, the body will not hold onto fats and will also release excess water on a daily basis. The wild rice removes excess plaque and cholesterol from the bloodstream. These foods can be eaten along with your normal daily diet. Juicing your own grapefruit and apples gives you the freshest juice possible with the most nutrients still intact.

Stay away from diet pills and fads. Not only are their claims primarily false, but they can physically harm your body. Water pills can be dangerous to the heart unless they are totally herbal and taken according to instructions.

Maintaining an exercise routine and eating properly are important, but these have nothing to do with weight-loss because the mind-pattern is everything. Controlling your thoughts is the only way to get the body that you desire.

Visualize yourself with your most perfect body. Then, put it in brown to release the thought to your Oversoul level for manifestation in physical reality. You can also use the following visualizations:

The Computer of the Mind Visualization

Create your personal file on the screen in royal blue.

Manipulate your body image into how you want it.

Save the file.

Put everything in brown to ground and bring it into the present.

The Violet Hose Visualization

With your mind, create a violet hose coming down from your Oversoul.

Use it to vacuum out all of the excess fat from your physical body.

Accelerate the process by visualizing a reddish-brown flame burning off the fat from specific parts of the body.

A very mentally powerful person is likely to have a thicker or heavier physical body than a mentally weak person. Keep in mind that despite the images that Hollywood and Madison Avenue project for you to look like, this is really not proper or real for the individual. You must look like who *you* are. You must be the most perfect version of that—even when your version has a larger waist or hips than the fashion industry says you should have.

The form you are right now is a reflection of your mind-patterns and experiences since the beginning of your existence. Change the thought and experiences, and the body shape changes—it is this simple!

Weight loss is not about losing pounds from your body, but rather about losing the weight of your burdens and fears. Instead of looking at how many pounds you have lost in a given time period, look at how much you have mentally released from your mind-pattern. Perhaps the title of this chapter should have been *Burden & Loss*. Burden-less and fear-less equals weight-loss.

Fertility

Fertility is fast-becoming an issue for many people around the world. Environmental, clothing, and financial factors as well as social burdens all contribute to a lower fertility rate in modernized and industrialized nations.

The real fertility issue is the mind-pattern people hold of not feeling creative or productive in life. There are also issues and fears of not wanting to recreate another version of self. With the science of cloning becoming increasingly mainstream, eventually fertility will no longer be an issue because there will be an easy, although extremely expensive, solution. And of course, you will one day hear that an artificial womb is an option.

Fertility can be physically enhanced as you work on the mind-patterns that create it. The following are suggested male and female protocols for enhancing fertility.

Male Fertility Enhancement

Take 500 mg of Siberian ginseng daily
Take 300 mg of saw palmetto herb daily
Take 700 mg of sarsaparilla herb daily
Take 50 mg of zinc daily
Take sea salt baths two-three times per week
Take 500-1200 mg of L-arginine daily
Put pale red in the root chakra every morning
Some men may need to take testicular glandular supplements for 90 to 120 days
Put castor oil over the scrotum nightly
Eat pumpkinseeds several times per week
Do not masturbate
Eat animal proteins daily

Female Fertility Enhancement

Take 850-1200 mg of wild yam root on days when not menstruating
Take 500 mg of black cohosh herb daily
Take 300 mg of aloe vera daily
Take sea salt baths four-six times per week
Eat animal proteins daily
Put castor oil over uterine area every night
Some women may need ovarian glandular supplement for 90 to 120 days
Put pale orange in sacral chakra every morning
Reduce strenuous aerobic exercises

Male & Female Fertility Enhancement Together

Start the following fourteen days after the start of the last menstrual cycle:

Have intercourse once per day, every other day, for ten days.

Visualize the pale orange Pregnancy Archetype in the uterus daily and during sexual activity.

Use one pregnancy archetype for each fetus. Using two at a time will result in twins, etc.

At the moment of orgasm, hold the thought that the female is pregnant. Place this thought in brown.

Be monogamous.

When both male and female follow the above procedures in exact detail for three to six months, a pregnancy will occur. The mind-pattern to support the physical work must also be in place, so do the mental work as well. Be fruitful and multiply!

Affirmations

Affirmations are an easy way to assist in the reprogramming of your mind-patterns so that you do not constantly repeat the same problems over and over again.

The best way to use affirmations is to monitor your thoughts. Every time a thought that puts you down or negates you in some way enters your mind, do the following:

Put a big brown "X" through the thought.

Immediately replace it with a positive, helpful thought.

Affirmations must always be positive and in the present tense. Do not use any negative words. Keep them simple. Use the following examples, and then create your own.

Creativity
I am <u>now</u> totally creative and productive in <u>all</u> areas of my life.

Depression
I am <u>now</u> happy and content with my life.

Direction/goals
I <u>now</u> take the most beneficial paths in life.

Fear
I only attract wonderful experiences to myself every day.

Finances
I <u>always</u> attract and use whatever money I need in life.

Health
I am <u>now</u> in perfect health.

Relationships
I <u>now</u> attract and maintain the most perfect relationships with other people

Residence
I <u>now</u> live in the most perfect home that matches my frequency.

Travel
All my journeys are easy and smooth.

Weight loss
I am <u>now</u> at my most perfect weight and shape.

Work/career
I <u>now</u> have the most perfect job and career, and I am paid my worth, its equivalent or better.

Mentally repeat affirmations often until they replace the old, non-serving mind-patterns. Sometimes it is helpful to write them down and look at them. Some people like to type them onto a computer, or post them where they can be seen frequently. Develop your own affirmations, tailoring them to meet your specific needs.

Oversoul
Communication

The Oversoul is the connection that everyone has to the God-Mind Totality. There is a direct link to this energy that is a foundational pattern to the existence of humankind. You can never lose this direct link or disconnect from it. The worst that can happen is that you lose your awareness of it.

The Oversoul contains many layers of existence and countless lifestreams that are part of its composition. The Oversoul is the switchboard of the God-Mind, focusing and spreading out the energies to many locations so that the God-Mind can know Itself under all circumstances.

The following is a simple visualization that helps to enhance the awareness levels and interactions of your soul-personality to its related Oversoul.

Oversoul Communication Preliminaries

Take two or three cleansing breaths.

Center your consciousness in royal blue at the pineal gland.

Balance your T-Bar archetype, or center the dot in the circle at your pineal gland, all in royal blue.

Oversoul Communication

Visualize a silver infinity symbol over the crown chakra.

Start talking to your Oversoul as if it is your friend/servant/ spouse/parent.

Always remember to thank it after you are finished with your conversations/demands/needs/etc.

Place yourself in brown after each session.

You can talk, yell, or cry to your Oversoul as often and long as you like. Your Oversoul is a larger part of you. Your Oversoul always listens and always responds. As you increase your frequency of Oversoul communication, you will notice that the responses back to you become faster and more understandable.

Some people like to "see" a bright star or sun over the infinity symbol as a representation of their Oversoul. Some people "see" an Angelic presence that is really an energetic level within the Oversoul structure. You will "see" or feel whatever your mind needs to use as an association and reference to your Oversoul.

You can ask your Oversoul to communicate with the Oversoul of another person. In this way, you are able to communicate or confront someone without being in his/her presence. You can send healings, speak to the departed, rearrange your life, or simply feel comforted by using this methodology. Oversoul communication is a wonderful way to see how powerful you really are, and to see who and what you really are.

Simple Prayer

Every day you are confronted with situations and feelings that require a quick interaction with the God-Mind within. There is no need for any elaborate communication since everyone is comprised of the God-Mind, and the God-Mind is within everyone. God-mind is as close as a thought.

There is a simple method for prayerful communication with the God-Mind that is quick and to the point, utilizing hyperspace principles. Proper prayer is about thanking as if everything is already received, because in the God-Mind, all is already done.

Hyperspace Prayer

Take a quick cleansing breath in through the nostrils, out through the mouth.

Center your consciousness in royal blue at the pineal gland.

Balance your T-Bar archetype, or center the dot in the circle at your pineal gland, all in royal blue.

Visualize the entire physical body engulfed in royal blue.

Surround the royal blue with a layer of purple (not violet) because purple is the color of prayer.

Surround everything with a layer of gold, as gold is the color associated with the God-Mind.

Thank the God-Mind for whatever it is that you are praying for, as if you have already received this.

For example, thank God for bringing you home safely, even if you are in the middle of a dangerous jungle. Or, thank God for allowing you to pay all of your bills, even if you are getting calls from creditors.

Complete your simple and to-the-point prayer.

Surround yourself in brown.

Use this affirmation—
All is accomplished now.

You can thank the God-Mind during this simple prayer for anything that you want. You can thank for as many things or events as you like. There is no limit.

After each prayer session, **know** that it is **done**. This is the proper way to pray—simply, quickly, and without any doubt of accomplishment!

Deprogramming Techniques

Everyone on this planet is programmed. The general population is programmed via subliminals in television and radio transmissions, movies, satellite bombardments, as well as carrier waves for cellphones, computers, and other electronic devices and broadcasts.

Globally, 1-2% of the population is specifically programmed for various functions. In the United States, 4-5% of the citizens are specifically programmed. More details are available in my video series on *Mind-Control, Programming and Deprogramming*.

The bottom line is that you live on a planet where if you do not take control of your own mind, someone else will. That someone else does not have your best interests in mind. The choice is yours. To assist yourself in reintegrating the fragmented compartments of your programming matrix, choose one or more of these initial and basic deprogramming techniques. Work through one at a time, keeping notes in a journal as you go so that you can begin to identify specific patterns, programs, and triggers.

Basic Deprogramming Preliminaries

Take two or three cleansing breaths.

Center your consciousness in royal blue at the pineal gland.

*Balance your T-Bar archetype, or center the dot in the circle
at your pineal gland, all in royal blue.*

Merger Visualization
*This is a standard deprogramming technique that leads
to more intricate work.*

Do the Basic Deprogramming Preliminaries.

*Visualize a brown merger symbol, as pictured above,
at your pineal gland.*

Hold this image at the pineal gland.

*Calmly and patiently see what surfaces into your
conscious mind.*

End by balancing your T-Bar archetype or circle with dot.

Place yourself in brown.

Write your experiences in your deprogramming journal.

Butterfly Visualization

This visualization is designed to identify any Monarch Programming within your matrix. Keep a separate journal for this exercise.

Do the Basic Deprogramming Preliminaries.

Visualize a Monarch Butterfly landing on your royal blue pineal gland and spreading its wings out.

Concentrate on the wings and see what comes into your mind.

Wherever this image takes you, always put a brown merger symbol over the scene in front of you.

End by putting the merger symbol in place of the butterfly.

Place yourself in brown.

Write your notes in your journal.

White Rabbit Visualization
This visualization identifies a matrix construct of Alice in Wonderland programming which is common to many people.

Do the Basic Deprogramming Preliminaries.

Visualize a white rabbit sitting on your royal blue pineal gland.

Mentally follow the rabbit's journey.

Stop at the first place the rabbit takes you to, even if the rabbit keeps going.

Look around at every detail, as this is the first compartment of your matrix that needs to be assimilated.

Put a brown merger symbol in the compartment,

Then, put a brown merger symbol in your pineal gland.

Place yourself in brown.

Make your notes in your journal.

Brown Shelf Visualization

The *Brown Shelf* is an excellent visualization designed to alleviate stress and worry. This visualization is especially helpful when you feel unfocused and burdened, or when you find it difficult to concentrate or sleep.

The Brown Shelf Visualization Preliminaries

Take two or three cleansing breaths.

Center your consciousness in royal blue at the pineal gland.

Balance your T-Bar archetype, or center the dot in the circle at your pineal gland, all in royal blue.

Place yourself in brown.

The Brown Shelf Visualization

See yourself in front of a wooden shelf of your own design—the kind does not matter.

Place all people, places, and events that trouble you on the shelf.

After you have placed everything on the shelf, visualize a pair of violet hands underneath the shelf.

Visualize the violet hands gently lifting the shelf up and away from you until it is no longer in view.

Know within that these troubles are permanently released.

Place yourself in brown.

Violet Balloon Visualization

The *Violet Balloon* visualization is an excellent method for releasing anything that bothers you, and for calming your nerves.

The Violet Balloon Visualization Preliminaries

Take two or three cleansing breaths.

Center your consciousness in royal blue at the pineal gland.

Balance your T-Bar archetype, or center the dot in the circle at your pineal gland, all in royal blue.

Place yourself in brown.

The Violet Balloon Visualization

See yourself writing down all your troubles and concerns on a piece of paper.

After you have written everything down, read your list.

Tie your list to the violet balloon.

Visualize the violet balloon carrying your list up and away from you until it is no longer in view.

Know within that these troubles are permanently released.

Place yourself in brown.

Janet's Articles

*"In True Reality, nothing within God-Mind
can ever abandon you."*

Abandonment

People with victim mentality issues often have abandonment issues. Feelings of abandonment often start at an early age with the perceived abandonment by a parent. Perhaps you were hungry, tired, wet, or cold, and no one came fast enough. Perhaps you did not get held or hugged at the exact moment when you wanted that physical contact. Perhaps you had a frightening nighttime experience and no one came to save you. Who abandoned you at an early age?

Once imprinted with this mind-pattern, most people are destined to constantly relive this imprinting over and over again, somehow looking for the door that opens and lets them escape this self-imposed prison. People with abandonment issues are quite creative in how they play this out. Who or what abandoned you growing up? A grandparent that died? A beloved pet that left and never came back? A high school trophy? A college scholarship? Friends that went different directions?

As an adult, who or what abandons you now? Has your family emotionally abandoned you (again!)? Have you had falling outs with trusted friends? Have spouses/companions repeatedly disappointed you? Has financial security peaked and left? Are once-thought attainable goals now seemingly out of reach? Have medical establishments failed to fulfill their promises of returning you to health?

How many times have you repeated the same abandonment cycle with different people, places, or things, but with the base mind-pattern always the same?

A mind-pattern of abandonment creates isolation issues, because if you are isolated and non-attached, then that means that no one/nothing can abandon you, right? Just isolate yourself every way that you can, and beat the game of abandonment! Sounds simple and easy…

In true reality, the origin of most abandonment issues goes beyond this lifeline and into the original "separation" of Self from Oversoul and God-Mind. There is a part of you that feels abandoned by the Original Parent. When you stretch your arms out you wonder why It is not there to hold and hug you, and to keep you safe; why It does not answer your many questions, why you are left here seemingly alone to suffer and struggle in pain.

The illusion of abandonment is actually an important part of compartmentalization. The illusion of the Original Abandonment was necessary to feel **completely** separate from your Oversoul and God-Mind so that you could play a part. Now that you have completed that phase, it is important for you to move through and beyond those feelings. The illusion of separation moves you into the false belief that you are abandoned. In True Reality, nothing within God-Mind can ever abandon you. You have it all.

The first step to moving "back" to God-Mind is the conscious awareness that you are not separate, **not** abandoned, and **never** can be. Remove the isolation issues to remove the abandonment issues. Use the following affirmations:

I release the need for the illusion of abandonment.

I now have all the support that I need—people, places, things, funding, mental prowess, physical health and strength, etc.

I am one with my Oversoul and God-Mind in conscious awareness.

I now have the total support of my Oversoul and God-Mind with me at all times, wherever I go.

The strength of my mind-pattern now pulls my Oversoul family to me.

My Oversoul family supports me and I support them; we are mutually interdependent.

Give thanks for the coming together in this reality of your Oversoul family. As the strength of your mind-pattern pulls them to you, and you to them, feel the support of your Oversoul and God-Mind. Feel the integration of your subpersonalities and alters. As the inner merging of Self takes place, realize that the outer world has no choice but to reflect this back to you. As your inner self merges into wholeness, your outer world does the same by reflecting a healthy, whole, interdependent, supportive outer world back to you.

As you release your self-imposed illusion and acceptance of separation from your Oversoul and God-Mind, you automatically release the mind-patterns of isolation and abandonment, along with any victim mentality that you might hold. The old mind-patterns have no place to take hold; they cannot stick or penetrate into your mind-pattern any longer. They simply fall away, and as they do so, this is your opportunity to return them to their source—your Oversoul and God-Mind, forever. You have been there, done that, and you do not need to do it again – time to explore bigger, better, and healthier mind-patterns.

"Read your body and it will tell you exactly what is going on in your mind-pattern."

Insulation

Planned insulation is working quite nicely. Everyone is falling quite easily into the trap of complacency and doldrums. Real food is gradually being replaced with foods of continually less and less substance. Value-added products are the best way that the agricultural industry can make the most profit on its investment. Take one grain of wheat and add a billion artificial ingredients, and the profit per acre immediately goes sky high.

Indigenous plants and animals are quickly disappearing through planned obsolescence. Whatever foods are native to your location are the most representative of your mind-pattern and most adequately meet the requirements of your body. This means seasonal foods as well as those that are available all year long. Just as a mother's milk changes hourly, daily, and monthly, to meet the growing needs of her baby, the Earth changes what she produces to meet the cyclic needs of her people.

Whenever you take a trip to the supermarket, it takes some skill and common sense to find real food that actually nourishes the body. There is plenty that will fill up your stomach, but how much of it actually feeds the body? Your stomach can be full, but your body starving for nutrition.

Taking care of your body is a real challenge. But before one casts too many stones at the outside sources, it is important to realize that the outside challenges cannot exist unless your mind-pattern creates them somewhere, someplace.

You have to go inside to find out why your real food sources for the body, i.e., the mind, are being eliminated. What part of you does not want real food in your diet? Many people supplement their aversion to their emotional/mental food with insulation on their physical bodies. This is merely an outpicturing of the internal mind-pattern.

Many people simply insulate with water. It takes a strong mind-pattern to take something with zero calories and build something with it. So if you think that you are weak because you carry extra weight and "cannot lose it," think again! You must be extremely powerful to create something with nothing!

You can choose to use that same strength to correct the existing mind-pattern instead of add to the imbalance. Go inside to find out what you are insulating against. Look at where the insulation is located on your body. Weight build-up on the hips and thighs represent insulation around sexuality and creativity. The buttocks represent insulation against the past (what are you carrying behind you??). Extra weight on the legs has to do with insulating against the future. Carrying extra insulation on the stomach has to do with digestion—what is it in your life that you do not want to digest?

Read your body and it will tell you exactly what is going on in your mind-pattern. Once you know, you have to decide if you can move forward without your coat of protective insulation. Sooner or later, this lifeline or another, the insulation has to come off. The soul-personality has eons of time to balance this out—what do you want to do about it now? Have you had enough of this mind-pattern yet, or do you still want to explore it?

When your mind-pattern is *really* ready for change and for diving into the part of self that creates insulation, then it will attract exactly what it needs to release the insulation. You will suddenly find that you have people in your life that support your release of insulation as well as *food* (not drugs and diet gimmicks), exercise routines (exercise your body just like you do your pets!), relationships, body workers, etc.

You can change your insulation issues anytime that you want. You just have to want to un-insulate more than you want to insulate. You must deal with all parts of self—not just a part here or there. Use this lesson to activate every tool that you know to get yourself moving forward. *Wanting* to make a change is a great start, but *wanting* the change is not the same as actually changing.

Sometimes you identify with the process so wholeheartedly that you do not want to complete the change because with what will you then identify? When the insulation is gone, what will be on the other side? Sexual issues? Relationship issues? Future issues? Health issues? Do you deserve a balanced sexual perspective? Fulfilling relationships? A positive future? Good health?

What if you lose your insulation, and you still do not find a mate? What if you lose the insulation and you put it back on? What if you need fewer trips to the doctor, then who will give you attention? What if you lose your insulation and you actually *are* sexy? What if your fantasies become reality—can you handle the positive? Will others be able to deal with the "new you"? Will you have to develop an entirely new repertoire of interactions with others? How much more of the old will have to drop off? The fear and victim questions go on ad infinitum. The insulation gives you an "acceptable" excuse—what will you use for an excuse without the insulation?

Most people have little tolerance to: dairy products, refined sugars, refined flours, refined grains, and artificial sweeteners, any chemical or artificially produced food. When the body does not tolerate something, it tries to protect itself by insulating, often using water to build a protective sheath around the cells that are affected. There are several products that you can use to help support water loss. Wild Yam helps balance the hormone system in women. Standard Process's AC Carbamide helps to feed the cellular wall so that water imbalances can self-correct. Standard Process also provides an adrenal support, as a stressed adrenal system can also add to water imbalance.

Use the following affirmations:

I release my excess insulation with ease.

I am at my desired weight with ease.

My support system is in place with ease.

I move forward with ease.

Think about all the lessons that your insulation taught you. Squeeze the lessons dry for every drop of knowledge that you possibly can, from your inner world to the reflections in the outer world. Release everything up to your Oversoul, and move up the evolutionary spiral of your soul-personality.

"Imagine a world where everything that you think automatically appears in front of you."

Outpicturing

Imagine a world where everything that you think automatically appears in front of you. If you think about living in a larger home, you are instantaneously within it. If you think of eating a wonderful food, it is automatically before you. If you think of visiting a beautiful location, you are suddenly there. If you imagine the perfect relationship, it automatically exists.

Your life and world would certainly be different. While this might sound entertaining and wonderful, you would have to live by different rules and regulations. For example, you would need to exercise more control over your thoughts so that your environment was not constantly changing moment by moment depending upon your moods and focus. In the same way, thoughts of different locations would leave you bouncing around the planet—perhaps even beyond. You might not be able to finish one meal before another one would appear, and so on.

And of course, what about the negative thoughts that cross your mind? Have you ever been so angry that you wished something terrible upon someone? In your "instantaneous" world, this would occur. Or, have you ever been so depressed that you would just like to curl up and die? This could happen as well. Back and forth, the world would not be a very constant place.

Because of the lack of control that most people have over their own thought processes, it is a good thing that most thoughts do not outpicture quite so quickly. However, each person is already outpicturing his/her deepest thoughts on a gradient level. That means the most conscious, constant, and focused thoughts are the ones that you see outpictured back to you on an everyday basis.

Most people do not realize it, as the world outpictured around you has depth and breadth, the same as your thoughts. Hidden thoughts, or less consciously acknowledged ones, outpicture differently than those at the forefront of your mind. For this reason, even though you may not recognize it, what you need most, physically outpictures the closest to you.

The stores, food, relationships, everything that you need on a daily, interactive basis is already around you as an outpicture of your thought process. These things automatically are drawn to you. The people who are around you, whether you know or like them, are the ones who most closely outpicture your mind-patterns regarding relationships, finances, self-worth issues, etc. Everything that exists in your world is an outpicture of your thoughts.

The deeper within that you go, the further away from home you must physically travel to experience that particular outpicturing. However, when you merge the hidden depths with the conscious, everyday awareness, even that which is hidden inside is now able to outpicture physically close to you.

Everyone who has Lyraen genetics has the ability to outpicture everything instantaneously because it was a less physical world where manipulation of matter was simply easier with the energy of thought. But the knowledge is now locked away, deep inside.

Most people do not think of accessing it because this knowledge is being artificially outpictured for them.

Television and movies, as well as computer and video games, are the largest sources of outpicturing at this time. If you live your life vicariously through these modalities, the most conscious levels of your existence feel satisfied. So, rather than explore space for yourself, watching someone else do so in a fictitious story satisfies you enough so that you forget that you that could do this yourself.

Lyraen genetics allow you to transform and shapeshift, but if you watch shows or read about others with these abilities, you experience through them. Your inherent need to express these genetics feels complete for the moment. Most people are satisfied to leave certain experience to science fiction novels,believing that the stories are impossible. Through these stories, they think that they have experienced as much of the impossible as can be experienced upon this planet. They may speak about these things with others, but the thought of actual experience is beyond the comprehension of most people.

This is why some people are known as "all talk." If you have an energy seed and you mentally nourish and feed it, it has a chance to grow. But if all you do is talk about it, the energy seed, or original thought, is consumed and the momentum to actually outpicture the thought is lost. In other words, if you experience it mentally in its totality, there is no need for you to bring that thought into fruition in this reality. Talking about it is simply enough to satisfy your desires. The energy seed is gone with the wind, and so is your desire to experience it further.

Mentally experiencing something and physically experiencing something is really one and the same. So, the powers-that-be lead you into outpicturing your fantasies so that you do not actualize them. This is one way of "stealing" your potential from you. Because you use their outpicturing, you do not take the time to outpicture for yourself.

For example, most people expect to age. One of the first things that you are imprinted with as a child is the average life span of a male and female human. This is reinforced through Social Security, pensions, and retirement plans the minute you enter the work force. People become a "senior citizen" somewhere between the ages of 55 and 65, with monetary incentives for declaring yourself one, thereby reinforcing the mind imprint. Forced retirement pushes many people into depression as they accept the "end of their usefulness."

The reality is that the human body is designed to regenerate itself and last for hundreds of years. But rather than create a body that does this, again, the average human looks to external sources that change the outer looks, but not the mind-pattern that created a failing body in the first place. So, even with plastic surgery and popular supplements like HGH, the body still fails regardless of how it looks.

As another example, think of a chiropractor. Because chiropractors exist, it is easy to make an appointment to adjust your back when it is out of place. This easily available resource takes away your impetus to learn how to hold your back into place by creating the correct mind-pattern. When you have a problem, you just go to someone outside of yourself who can fix it. Using a chiropractor as a window of opportunity is great, but becoming dependent upon one takes away your chance to develop your own innate healing, self-correcting, and self-balancing skills.

Necessity is often the "mother of invention." But if you are fed a constant stream of new experience, you forget to think about what you would like to experience. You have no need to invent or create "outside the box." Your every mental need is met before you even realize that a need exists. This is because your "needs" are artificially created and then met. You follow "the yellow brick road" wherever it takes you, thinking that all your desires are satisfied.

Most people become so accustomed to using the outpictures of others that either they forget that they can do it, or they simply never reach the realization of their full potential. Continue to use these quickly changing times as the impetus that drives you further into actualizing your full potential. Settle for nothing less than the Triad Partnership of Self, Oversoul, and God-Mind. Push your way into your inner depths so that you are in control of what you outpicture rather than allowing others to be one step ahead of you. When you see what they offer, do not change yourself to match their misleading outpicturings. Instead, operate from the internal to correctly allow the external to outpicture you, rather than vice versa. Think about it.

*"Most of what and how you will experience the rest of
your life is often determined by the time that you
are five-years-old based upon these imprints."*

Parental Issues

Most people have "parent issues." This is understandable,
considering that these are usually the first people who imprint
the conscious mind. Most of what and how you will experience
the rest of your life is often determined by the time that you are
five-years-old based upon these imprints.

Most people usually respond to their early years in one of two
ways. The first way is to try to control other people or situations.
As a child, these people felt powerless, or, "out of control." To
correct this imbalance, the suppressed childhood emotions within
the adult now assumes "control," regardless of the consequences
to others.

If one parent was particularly bossy and you felt "bossed around"
you will in your adult life "boss others around." If you felt
abandoned, you may abandon those around you. Now, you are
the one doing the bossing and/or abandoning. This gives a sense
of power and control. This is how negative cycles perpetuate.
Whatever was done to you, you can now do to someone else. The
suppressed childhood emotions are now unleashed and
expressing. This part of you is thrilled to now have control.

If you felt powerless as a child, you will find a situation where you feel powerful. This can often be seen in the workplace, where some supervisors wield their power like swords. Or, where one employee manipulates one against another-all power plays resultant from people who feel powerless and must at some point work it out so that he/she does have power, even if it is gained by being devious, sneaky, and underhanded.

The difficulty with this type of behavior is that most likely others are hurt in the process. This is a reflection of the hurt that was done to you, and that you are avoiding. So, you hurt others over and over again in an attempt to reconcile that hurt with the offending parent. This particular emotional part of you virtually stopped maturing as a young child. Since that young child had no choice, it suppressed those feelings. The child could not consciously do anything but go along with the parental program. Because it does not have the tools to know any better, that hurt, angry child now feeds the cycle.

The second primary way of responding to parental issues is to bring someone into your life who repeats the same type of behavior as your parent. If your parent emotionally and/or physically abandoned you, you will bring someone in who does this to you, over and over again. This could be a spouse, child, friend, relative, or coworker. By bringing someone else in to continue to play the "parent role" there is a part of you, s pecifically the part that was "injured" at that age level, who is trying to work this out through anyone who will assume the role.

Some people willingly assume the role, while others do not. If you cannot find a willing participant to assume the role of, for example, your mother, you may subconsciously target a female who is close to you and then put that role upon her. You may "attack" her in many ways as you continue to try to come to terms with your own mother. This can make life even more uncomfortable for the recipient of such attacks. These surrogates usually have a victim mentality mind-pattern that provides the entrée for these types of attacks.

Even the time that was spent in utero begins the mind-imprinting process. If you felt wanted and loved, this is how you at least begin your life. What happens after that continues your saga. If your mother was confused, frightened, or perhaps just did not want a baby, this becomes an added emotional trauma that the soul-personality has chosen.

If you were adopted, there are often feelings of abandonment. Emotionally, you may wonder why your birth mother "did not want you" and infer that this means lack of love. This may or may not be the case. After being within the warm safety of the womb for so many months, and then being torn away from it into the arms of strangers creates a major trauma for a tiny newborn. This may promote a lifetime of abandonment issues, or a person who continually tries to develop a "safe" environment to replicate the one that he/she felt torn from. This "safe" environment may lead to a lifetime of seclusion, isolation, and even stagnation. Or, a wanderer who never really feel like he/she belongs anywhere.

Everyone is basically "same song, different verse." Your mind-imprints basically stem from your primary caregivers. Remember that you chose your parental figures as the people who most reflected your own mind-pattern at the moment of your conception. Once attached to these people, you impart your own name frequency to them, so if you have always disliked your name, you need to look at that. If you have significantly changed your name, this changes your birth frequency and alters the capability of the soul-personality to fully express and actualize its potential in this lifeline. Nicknames, assumed names, using a middle name for a first name, all shorten or change the birth frequency, consequently altering its expression. Names assumed through marriage and adoption may or may not enhance the birth frequency.

If you do not have anything to do with your parents, you need to take a look at this. If you do not like them, for any reason, these are lessons yet unlearned. If they generally annoy or upset you, again, study them, for they are your first and foremost primary teachers about who and what you are, and why you are even here. You chose them, you chose your birth name, you chose the location where you were born. All this is set up via the Oversoul level so that the soul-personality will have the opportunity to evolve in some way, shape, or form. What did you set up to learn in this lifeline? Why did you choose your parents? Are you avoiding them now, and why? Are you repeating their behavior? Are you becoming them?

First, you need to go back to the age when your soul-personality allowed them to imprint it for this lifeline-usually, by the age of five or under. Determine the underlying issues that you have with your parent(s), such as physical and/or emotional isolation, abandonment, betrayal, control, feeling powerless, lack of nurturing, etc. Review your current life situation to determine how you are trying to work these issues out, and with/through whom or what situation. Once you recognize that you are recreating a part of your childhood, then you can deal with it.

Place the parent figure above your head up into your Oversoul. Allow the child who consciously did not have the tools to express his/her feelings at the time to yell, scream, kick, hit, punch, or whatever is necessary to remove these leftover emotional feelings from childhood. Feel the flow of this energy moving up from your auric field, up through the base of your spine and out the top of your head. Clean the emotions out of your system and give them all to your Oversoul.

As you clean, ask that your Oversoul deliver this message to the parent's Oversoul, and from there on to the parent. The parent will get the message in accordance with the wishes of his/her Oversoul. Whenever any of these types of feelings arise, repeat the exercise. This removes the mind-imprint from you, gives it to your Oversoul, cleans you up, and does not attack the other person.

As the imprint removes from you, you release the need for the continual "trying" of working it out with someone else. Now you are working it out with the person with whom you should be working it out-your parent, recognizing that this person is ultimately a reflection of yourself.

As the excess emotions are drained from your auric field, you can ask that your Oversoul relay any information from the parent to you via his/her Oversoul. Discuss this with the parent in the Oversoul space above your head. You may learn something. Now you are in a mind-frame to objectively observe, listen, and learn. As the emotions and logic (left-brain/right-brain) come into balance, you are finally ready to release your particular lesson back to your Oversoul, from whence it originated. Now, you can forgive them for their part, and yourself for your part.

As the excess emotions are released from your field, and you become cleaner and clearer, your relationships can elevate themselves into their potential. This is how you "assimilate" that mind-pattern so you can evolutionize and work on something else.

You will know that you have truly assimilated this mind-pattern when you can be in your parents' space without judgement, criticism, or emotional reaction-when they can no longer "push your buttons." In this way, you rise "through" the energy of this experience instead of residing "in" the energy of the experience.

Now, as an observer, you have an appreciation for what you learned and for the people who took the time to teach you. You took a lot of time to set this experience up for yourself, so make the most of the opportunity. If you do not learn what you need, you will continually recreate it until you "get it" and it will manifest and magnify until you are myopically focused and forced into it.

Rather than avoid the parental experience, move in and through it. You will be glad that you did when you get to the other side, as this will mean another step in the evolutionary process of your soul-personality.

"I forgive myself for all that I did, consciously and unconsciously, to allow the situation to occur."

Six Steps To Forgiveness

Almost everyone has forgiveness issues because somewhere along the way, in your mind, someone "did" something to you that you just cannot quite get over. You may even logically understand the situation, but emotionally you may be harboring bits and pieces of hurt, frustration, doubt, bitterness, and possibly even hatred that seem to be wedged inside.

The positive side of these negative emotions is that whatever you learned, you do not forget! And most likely, you promise yourself that you will never repeat the experience. However, until you completely understand and release the experience from your auric field, there is a high likelihood that you *will* repeat the experience in one form or another until you "get" the lesson. Keep in mind that on some level of awareness, you agreed to the situation for some reason so that your soul-personality could learn and grow.

To complete your experience and completely remove it from your auric field so that you do not have to continue to repeat the experience, you may want to use to following six steps.

1. Allow all suppressed emotions to express on the Oversoul level

Place the person with whom you have issues above your head up into your Oversoul. Allow all parts of yourself that harbor unexpressed emotions, such as hurt, frustration, doubt, bitterness, and hatred to freely express these feelings. Allow these parts to yell, scream, hit, punch, or do whatever is necessary to the person in your Oversoul space. This relieves and removes the existing leftover energy from you and experientially passes it up to your Oversoul.

Ask your Oversoul to deliver your message, in whatever form that takes, to the other person's Oversoul. Tell your Oversoul to ask his/her Oversoul to pass this message on to the individual in the appropriate way at the appropriate time. In this way, the person will receive the message in a way that he/she can actually "hear" as well as understand on some level of awareness.

2. Hear the other person's side on the Oversoul level

After you have drained yourself of the existing emotions, you are now ready to hear the other person's side of the story. Ask your Oversoul for a response from the other person via his/her Oversoul. Your Oversoul will pass this message on to you. Remember that you only communicate with your own Oversoul, never anyone else's. Your Oversoul is the filter through which all communication passes so that *you* can "hear."

3. Understand what he/she taught you

Objectively review what you learned from this person. Why did you allow this lesson in your life? What part of you needed the balance that this person brought to your life? Nothing can happen unless there is some level that attracts and allows an experience.

4. Thank the person for taking the time to teach you

On the Oversoul level, thank the person for taking the time to teach you. Understand that he/she is busy with his/her own work. He/she took time to stop long enough on his/her journey to be a part of your play so that you could learn about yourself.

5. Forgive him/her

Use the following affirmation:

I forgive you for all that you did to me, both consciously and unconsciously.

If you cannot say this and mean it, then you need to go back to Step #1, as most likely you are still harboring negative emotions toward that person. These emotions will never harm the other person, only yourself. Continue to repeat the steps until you can say the above affirmation and actually mean it.

6. Repeat with Self

Most likely, you are angry with yourself on some level for allowing the situation to have occurred. Some part of you thinks that you could have/should have prevented the situation. Put yourself up into the Oversoul level and do the releasing work as described in Step #1, and so forth. When you come to Step #5, use the following affirmation:

I forgive myself for all that I did, consciously and unconsciously, to allow the situation to occur.

As with others, if you cannot say this statement and mean it, continue going back to Step #1 until you can.

Whatever you hold onto prevents you from moving forward. This is because you cannot experience something new until you have emptied out the old. You only have room for "x" number of experiences within your auric field. If you are filled up, so to speak, you must pour something out to prepare for the new to enter. Think about your choices, and the results of each. What path can you take that will quicken the journey toward your goal? Who is blocking your path? Is it you?

*"The original frequency, of which you are a part,
is too strong to be held in just one body."*

Soulmates?

Many people search for their "soulmate," usually defined as the "one person" with whom they can share the rest of their life in bliss and ecstasy; who will understand and appreciate them more than any other person in the entire world.

The delusion is that there is only "one" soulmate. Technically, there is One Soul—God-Mind, so **anyone** is a potential "soulmate." Looking for a "soulmate" as defined above is a distraction. The following affirmation is a more accurate request:

***I give thanks for a relationship with the (man/woman) who
most closely matches my frequency.***

You have a specific unique frequency that originated when your soul-personality came forth out of your Oversoul. Simply put, your Oversoul is the point of origin from which your specific frequency was birthed out of God-Mind. At that point, your soul-personality did not exist as you now know it. As the frequency descended into physical reality, the frequency split and split and split until it was fragmented enough to fit into a physical body.

The original frequency, of which you are a part, is too strong to be held in just one body. It needs many bodies to hold the full frequency and function in this, and other, realities simultaneously. This explains why every soul-personality emanating from one Oversoul has a different function.

Consider the physical body as an analogy. The body has one base frequency, but a liver has a little different frequency than a kidney, etc. All body parts from the same body have the same base frequency, but one does not replicate another's function. In the same way, each frequency split from your Oversoul acquired its own individuality depending upon its function, still never replicating the function of any other frequency split. This gives its frequency its individuality.

The closer that another soul-personality is to your own split from the original frequency, the more your basic frequencies have in common. Again, using the body as an analogy, the large intestine and the small intestine have more in common than the large intestine and the brain. The large intestine and the brain belong to the same unit, they have the same base frequency, and they are both necessary for the experience of the body. This is why it is important to ask your Oversoul to bring to you the person who most closely matches your own frequency.

This similarity in function provides the compatibility that you seek. However, just because you find a compatible frequency, you still have to work with and through the individual experiences of the frequency. Many people fall into the delusion that when they find a compatible frequency the relationship will go smoothly.

Because your Oversoul does not do the same thing twice, the two of you most likely will have a variety of traits that may be diametrically opposed. In addition, the pull of the other person will be so strong you will understand "love" within an entirely new dimension. Because the other person is so much a part of yourself, you will love that person with the depths of your soul. Within this type of relationship, you have the potential for limitless fulfillment within every part of your being. On the other hand, this also means that your vulnerability and the potential to be hurt increases exponentially.

Knowing all of this, when you look for a compatible frequency, you may decide to ask specifically for your twin flame or other half. A twin flame refers to the last split before you entered your original body in physical reality—first there was one, now there are two. An "other half" is an even further refinement. This means that it takes two bodies to hold one soul-personality.

Whether you actually unite with your twin flame or other half in this lifeline is entirely up to your Oversoul. In the Eternal Now, there is no such thing as time. You may spend many lifelines apart while each of you garner separate experiences that add to the whole. One may be in body while the other one is not. You may live on different parts of the world with entirely different life styles; or even in different realities. Do not force the timing. How do you find the one person incarnated on this Earth at this time who is the closet split to your own soul-personality? Ask your Oversoul to help you find this person. Use the following affirmations:

I am now together with my twin flame or other half—
whichever is the most appropriate for me—
or his/her equivalent.

I ask that I be made ready for him/her and he/she be made
ready for me.

It is important that you realize that each relationship you have provides the opportunity for balance. Each relationship is a reflection of yourself and as you move through it, you continually draw closer and closer reflections of yourself. Put another way, you come closer and closer to similar soul-personalities with similar frequencies until your mind-pattern automatically attracts first your twin flame, and finally your other half.

If you push your timing and ask for your twin flame or other half "no matter what," there is no guarantee that you will even recognize each other, much less have a decent relationship. Even though the deepest parts of yourselves match frequencies, the outer layers will cloud this from your vision.

As an analogy, think of a knife that you use to make a tuna sandwich with pickles. The knife becomes covered with tuna, mayonnaise, and pickles. When you look at it, it may be so covered with tuna, mayonnaise, and pickles, that you may not even realize that it is a knife. This is really true of almost every person. Most do not even realize that they are not the tuna, mayonnaise, and pickles. They forget that they are the really the knife beneath it all, albeit hidden from view.

This is why your affirmation work is so important. These words are the tools that pull you out of the delusion of what you think you are and into the reality of what you really are. Be patient and release your need for self-sabotage so that you can bring forth someone into your long-term picture with whom you are willing to go the distance on all levels, both positive and negative. Remember, anyone can get along when times are good. The test of a true relationship is not how you get through the good times, but how you get through the bad times.

*"The world around you is one giant tone;
a wonderful symphony."*

Toning

The world around you is one giant tone; a wonderful symphony. Everything has a tone, from a blade of grass to a cup on your table. Everything tones in harmony or in a cacophony. The placement of everything in the world affects the tone of the world.

Even language is a form of toning that affects the body and ultimately the Earth. Listen to the tone of English, and compare it to Oriental languages, and then to Middle Eastern Languages, etc. Each dialect within a language group has a different tone. Think of the romance languages, as an example. Raise your consciousness up above the Earth and look down upon it. In your mind, "see" the tones that emit from the different parts of the Earth simply from the language being spoken.

Each time that you feel something, whether you verbally express it or not, there is an accompanying tone that imprints upon your mind-pattern, your auric field, and ultimately your body. Tones come before words. After you express the tone, you find a word to label the tone. Think of the tones that you create every day:

Nervous—teeth chatter
Cold—brrr
Angry—grrr
Tired—sigh
Excited/frightened—scream
Happy—laughter
Upset—sobbing

You can "play" your day like a musical instrument through tones. Think about how you felt when you first got up in the morning, the contentment you felt after breakfast, the frustration of driving to your job, the rush through lunch, the busyness of the afternoon, driving back home, making/eating dinner, rushing here or there, or lounging in front of the television until bedtime. Make a tone when you think of each one of these scenarios. Now, you have your day expressed via tone.

You can express your entire life through tone if you are patient enough to express the tones of each day and year of this existence. You can do this because everything that you feel creates a tone within. Extrapolating upon this same principle, you can express your simultaneous existences through tone.

You can do the same with your body. Each body part has a unique sound to it. Play the sound of your body, using your vocal cords to match the tone of a specific part. When you "tone" the sounds of your feet, what do you see, feel, and/or hear? What stories are hidden in the song of the feet? Where have they carried you in this lifeline as well as in others? To which foreign lands? Have they been barefoot or shoed? What kind of shoes have they worn? Has their path been easy or difficult?

Move up through your legs and up into each part of your body, thinking about the mind-pattern that it contains. Allow it to express itself through tone. Listen as you create the sound that matches the specific tone of the body. Maybe some of the tones are not pleasing. But then again, maybe some of the experiences they hold have not been pleasant.

Remember that the body is created around the mind-pattern, and the tones simply express this. As you replicate and harmonize the tones of the body, you create a song/message/expression/communication which is no longer silent to your conscious mind. As these buried communications are finally allowed to express, they can be released up to your Oversoul. As the tones come forth, pass them up to your Oversoul via your inner eye. As you do this, ask for any specific information that you need to pass before your inner eye.

After you allow the body, auric field, and mind-pattern to express their current states, you can then use the tones to break up stagnant mind-patterns through tone. Start with your feet, and again move up your body, shattering with tone anything that is stagnant and in need of movement. Let it all come out. Let that tone rip, roar, and roll out of you. Feel your entire cellular structure vibrating, shaking, and quaking as old patterns shatter and move up to your Oversoul.

Now, create the tones to help your body, auric field, and mind-pattern self-correct and balance. Finally, replicate the new tone that your body, auric field, and mind-pattern now express.

Each person has a tone. You can "play" the tone of any person, place, or thing simply by harmonizing your voice with whatever already exists. As you harmonize, your frequency begins to match the frequency of your target. Using your Oversoul connection, ask your Oversoul to explain the frequency to you. The explanation may come via colors, pictures, words, or the cleanest, clearest way of all—simply via knowing by knowing.

Toning is one way that indigenous peoples gain their knowledge. They harmonize with their environments mentally, spiritually, and yes, "musically." This is why their ceremonies often include song and dance. They "enter" the frequency of whatever it is that they choose to communicate with and/or explore.

For example, if the Native Americans want to hunt buffalo, their "dance" or movements are actually the movements of the buffalo frequency in and through them. Their "singing" or tones are actually the tones of the buffalo frequency. Entering into the frequency of the buffalo and harmonizing with it allows them to communicate with the frequency, i.e., they now speak the "language of the buffalo."

To prepare for a hunt, for example, they enter into the buffalo frequency. They assume its identity and become one with it. As they do so, they automatically connect and are a part of its group mind. In effect, they "become" buffalo. Once within the frequency they "know" the location of the nearest herd, they "know" which buffalo they are to take for their food, and what they take, they take with the permission of the frequency. This is why the hunters knew if the hunt would be successful, as well as where to go.

This also explains the recent display of the British Royals' interest in Africa. They start harmonizing with the frequency of Africa, even assuming its identity, as Britain's queen assumes the frequency of an African queen. Once in Africa's frequency, they become a part of its frequency. Within the frequency, they can explore it, and in their case, change and exploit it to their own benefit.

This is the same way that programming is carried out with those that are specific targets. The powers-that-be replicate the frequency of their target. Because the target emits a specific tone, he/she does not realize when the same tone is piggybacked upon his/her tone from the outside. This artificially created tone is stealthily, patiently, and gradually inserted into the tone of the target. Once inserted, other artificial tones are gradually piggybacked onto it, and just like a needle pulling a thread, the artificial tones go into the target. Without conscious awareness, the target does not even realize that this is done.

The target's own tone is slowly changed to match the artificial tones. In order to effectively change something, it must be done from the inside. This is exactly what occurs in every instance. Every target is infiltrated from the inside in such a subtle way that the target does not consciously have a clue as to what is happening. And, the plan is not a short term one. Every infiltration is carefully and meticulously planned and carried out over a period of years, sometimes decades, sometimes centuries.

Professional con artists use the same technique. First, they match the tone of their targets. Whatever the target wants or needs, the con artist provides. Step by step, they develop a harmony until the target's tone is infiltrated. At that point, the con artist easily takes what he/she wants often before the target realizes that anything even happened. Anything can be "infiltrated" and exploited in this way. But those that exploit shall someday have to face the consequences of their choices.

Exploration through tone allows one access to all kinds of fascinating information. For example, a map of the oceans can be created through sound alone. You can harmonize with the water frequency, then simply follow it on its course. Without ever leaving your home, you can "travel" with the water tone, or frequency, to determine where water meets land, where it is deep and where it is shallow, as well as find hidden perils. You can determine what is beneath the water, from caverns and sand to rocks and volcanoes. You can determine what swims within the water and where to fish. Tone is one method of exploration used by sentient beings since "time" began.

Think of the tones of war; of the warrior spirit; of the infamous battle cry. Even soldiers tone while in training—think of the "songs" that they tone during their long hours of marching. The powers-that-be seek to change the tone of the Earth herself to harmonize with the tones of war. The powers-that-be came to power because of their warrior spirits. This is what is within them. They are changing the morphogenetic grid of the Earth with their crop circles, among other things, to install a warrior spirit through a warrior tone. They are artificially inserting a war tone into the grid of the Earth so that every living thing feels, hears, and resonates with it. This artificial warrior tone is thusly imprinted into everything that exists within this reality.

And, people accept this warrior tone, easily harmonizing with it. Why? Because this tone originates from the people themselves. How so? These tones are artificially forced out when the populace is purposely provoked into emitting violence, rage, anger, hurt, and frustration. Even these emotions emitted for a "good" reason (i.e., the injustices of the world) are still part of the same tone. The tone is taken, forced into the morphogenetic grid, held there, and force-fed back into the population at the whim of the controllers via the touch of a button.

This takes us back to the needle pulling the thread. When the tone comes from you, it eventually has to return to you. It is yours. When it is unleashed, there is a part of you that recognizes and accepts it. However, piggybacked onto your tones are artificial enhancements that are plugged right into you once the insertion takes place. These enhancements exacerbate what already exists within, ballooning your warrior tones out of "normal" proportions.

For those of you who read Book 3 from my *In Search of Yourself series*, there is a chapter called "Recycling Your Energy." Briefly summarized, this chapter explains how all experiences (which come from color, tone, and archetype) originate from your Oversoul and are destined to return there. This is why it is important to do your release work at the end of each day and night—to keep what you no longer need flowing up to your Oversoul so it can give you new, vertical experiences which in turn keep you moving upward on your evolutionary spiral.

Catholicism is one example where the priests step in to take on the part of the Oversoul. Why do you think "good" Catholics go to confession? To circumvent their color, tone, and archetypes to the priests and away from their own Oversouls, thus empowering the Catholic Church and weakening the parishioners.

In the same way, when you do not release to your Oversoul, but rather out into the environment, the tones you emit are "free game" to anyone who wants to utilize them. Since you do not properly clean them up yourself, anyone who understands energetics can "borrow" them. They cannot really permanently take the tones, but the tones can be artificially transmuted until you recognize what is occurring and reclaim them.

The powers-that-be imprint the mind of the youth with warrior games and movies. They are creating a global army with one mind-pattern that harmonizes with the warrior tone that they are artificially inserting into the frequency of the Earth. Their intentions are to eventually take this global army out to conquer other planets. Basically this planned global army is imprisoned with ropes of bondage created from tones emitted from their own mind-patterns. These ropes psychically exist, consisting of shape, color, form, weight, and tone.

The Illuminati are clever. In their minds, there is no stopping them. They understand the energetics of this reality. They have money, but money is not power. Money is only a tool of power. Knowledge is power, and that is what the masses have given them. You can use tone to change this. You can help to harmonize the Earth into something greater than this. You can use tone to harmonize, replicate, and essentially enter into the frequency of the powers-that-be and learn *their* "secrets." You can use your tones to "shatter" the frequencies that are already installed into the collective unconscious, as well as into the Earth herself. You can use the tones to harmonize yourself so that your outer world has no choice but to harmonize itself to you. You can use tone to call back any part of your tone that is held by someone else.

Explore the world of tone and add it to your cache of hyperspace tools. Add it to the collective unconscious in such a way that the powers-that-be do not win. Remember, it is **they** who are afraid of **us**, and that is why they seek to control us. There are more of us than of them, and collectively we are more powerful. They play mental games with us—it is time to beat them at their own game. Being in fear of them plays right into their hands and is ultimately ludicrous. This is the biggest "hoodwink" of all.

Let us now release our victim mentality and acknowledge the strength that is inherent within us, anchored to the greatest strength that exists—Oversoul and God-Mind.

I am anchored in the strength of my Oversoul and God-Mind.
In and with this strength, I add the tones of my voice to
forever change the course of "planned" history.
It is done.

*"Everybody already knows everything –
this is simply a matter of where you choose
to focus your attention."*

Know By Knowing

What would you like to know? Whatever you decide, recognize that you already know! Somewhere, part of yourself instantaneously is aware of the answer as soon as you ask the question. The challenge is to be able to focus on the part of yourself that has the answer and bring it forward into your conscious mind in this reality at the moment you desire.

Sound complicated? Initially, perhaps. But the reality is that it is extremely simple. First, you understand the basic concept, then you build on this basic concept to accomplish your goals.

***Everybody already knows everything –this is simply a matter
of where you choose to focus your attention.***

For example, right now, sitting exactly as you are, you know more information than you could possibly ever state. You know your name, age, date and place of birth, address, country, phone number, race, family members, and a myriad of other personal details.

You know that you are sitting at a computer. You know what room you are in, what direction you are facing, how the furniture is arranged, what the furniture pieces are called, the colors around you, time of day or night, if the light is off or on, room temperature, etc., etc. When you take the time to consciously label all that you know right now, in this moment, it is pretty amazing.

Keeping this in mind, you begin to get an idea of the vastness of all that you already know. In True Reality, you already know everything about everything. If you took the time to consciously label the details of everything that you know and of which you are already aware, it would drive you crazy! You would be in a constant state of overload!

Being able to "not know" in its own way is a blessing in disguise. "Not knowing" allows you to focus on what the soul-personality expects to accomplish right now. Some people are not able to blot out this vastness of information. They do not know how to focus on what is only in front of them. They receive their information "involuntarily."

Most people have at least one involuntary paranormal experience. This means that when they least expect it, something happens that allows them to have access to another dimension and/or reality. Some people have many involuntary paranormal experiences, which means that they quite often have to deal with other dimensions and/or realities, all the while maintaining their focus in this one. This is not necessarily an easy task.

Some people have so many involuntary, overwhelming experiences that they are not able to reconcile them with this reality. Many of these people are labeled mentally insane and wind up in mental institutions, oftentimes drugged to try to help their minds focus on the here and now. These people actually see, hear, and feel things that others cannot because they involuntarily focus where others are not able. With proper guidance, these people could be taught to understand their particular situation and become functioning members of society.

Usually, this guidance is not available and these people live their lives misdiagnosed and misunderstood.

You can achieve a satisfactory balance between "not knowing" and "involuntary" experiences. You can learn to focus your attention in such a way that you receive your information "voluntarily," meaning that you can get what you need to know when you need to know it without disrupting the overall goal of the soul-personality in the here and now.

Once you recognize what you already know, you simply begin building on that concept. Pick up any object, and focus on what you already know about that object. For example, a cotton towel. Trace it back to its origins, step by step. You can trace it back to the farmer planting the cotton seed if you like. You can trace it back farther, to the store where the farmer purchased it, or how it even came to be in the store. You can learn more and more and more about that towel than you ever imagined when you take the time to focus and follow its energy thread. See how much you already know? You are not being "psychic" you are simply functioning in a state of knowing.

In the same way, everyone already sees auras, archetypes, simultaneous existences, etc. It is simply a matter of where you focus in physical realty that determines what you see and what you consciously know. Most people simply do not realize that they *can* focus on these things. They block this information so that they can focus on what is important to them at the moment.

Think about a person with whom you are well acquainted. Label all the things you know about this person–from name, age, and date of birth to likes, dislikes, emotional makeup, physical structure, health, strengths, weaknesses, etc. Again, the list can go on and on. When you stop to label all that you know, you realize that it takes longer to create your list than just to ***know*** these things. Now, think about what this person says versus what he/she does. How do these differ? Or do they? For example, they may say that they are in a satisfying personal relationship with someone, but what do you *know* from your observations? Perhaps they tell you that they are upset over a physical condition but you *know* that they create it for attention. Look at that! You read his/her mind-pattern!

Where did that mind-pattern come from? Follow the energy thread, just like you did with the cotton towel. Think about the obvious–parents. Follow the thread there. What do you know about parents? Do they have a separate "feel" than siblings? Does a mother figure "feel" different than a father figure? Where does the energy thread go from there?

When did the mind-pattern begin? Follow the energy thread to potential age groups. What does a twenty-year old "feel" like? Or a teen? Or a toddler? Or an infant? Each group has a whole different "feel," or frequency, to it. If you can feel the difference in the groups, you are beginning to understand frequencies.

Never pry or investigate anyone for curiosity. If you do, either you will automatically shut down or you will open yourself up to allow others to do the same to you. Always ask permission via the involved Oversouls. Follow the energy thread up to your Oversoul, and work vertically, never horizontally. Confirm everything with your source. Make wise decisions about where you choose to focus. Recognize that you already know everything. Be grateful that you can learn to function in a voluntary state of knowing by knowing. All you need to do is practice in conscious awareness!

*"Your Oversoul is where **you** come from."*

What Exactly *Is* An Oversoul?

What exactly *is* an Oversoul? Your Oversoul is where *you* come from. As an analogy, think of God-Mind as your grandmother/ grandfather. Out of God-Mind came smaller portions of energy called Oversouls. Think of an Oversoul as your mother/father.

What does an Oversoul look like? Each Oversoul is an energy mass of intelligence. For visualization purposes, you can think of it as looking like the sun on a bright day.

What function does an Oversoul perform? Your Oversoul provides an intermediary link between God-Mind, an extremely vast energy, and you, a small portion of that vast energy. Your Oversoul is a type of buffer between yourself and God-Mind. For example, you could not plug your kitchen toaster directly into an electric generator at a dam. The powerful wattage from the electric generator would be too powerful and would burn out the toaster.

All of your experiences originate from your Oversoul. Your Oversoul sends out your experiences by casting out a net of energy. You pull that net of energy into yourself as you experience. Then, you can choose to hold onto that energy and continue to repeat the same experience, or you can consciously choose to give that energy back to your Oversoul, so that the energy can be cleaned up and recast into new and different experiences.

Is an Oversoul the same as my Higher Self? "Higher self" can mean many things, but an Oversoul is your specific birth point out of God-Mind.

How do I contact mine? Your Oversoul is a constant. You are always connected no matter where you are or what form you take. You are always connected whether or not you are consciously aware of this. Your Oversoul recognizes you by your frequency – a vibration that is unique to you.

How do I develop awareness of my connection? First of all, visualize a clear, elasticized channel that connects the top of your head up to your Oversoul. Using your breath as a tool, exhale your breath up through the top of your head, up through this channel, all the way up into your Oversoul. Inhale it back down the channel. Exhale it back up, then bring the breath back down. If you see or feel any dark accumulated debris, use your breath as a scrub brush to clean it out. As you move your breath up and down, pass the loosened debris on up the channel to your Oversoul. Your Oversoul always stays clear and clean.

How do I know when I make contact? With your hands, feel the space that sits above your head. This is the area that contains your thoughts. You must use your breath, or consciousness, to push up past your own thoughts to get into the space that holds your Oversoul. In the beginning, it may be difficult to know that anything is happening. Your communications may be so subtle that you are not able to separate them from your own thoughts and feelings. That is why it is important to push up above the space that contains your own thoughts. The more you use the channel, the more perceptive you are to the communications that flow down it.

How will my Oversoul communicate with me? You will learn the language of your own Oversoul, which is the language of feeling. You will learn to know by knowing. You will recognize how much you already know, then build on that knowledge. Once you know the language of your own Oversoul, ask your Oversoul to communicate with all other things for you, then bring that information to you. Your work becomes much easier, because instead of having to learn the language of everyone and everything, you only need this one, simple language.

Will this change my perspective on life in general? Moving your energy up and down, rather than back and forth, means that you look at life from above rather than horizontally through your own accumulated vibratory imprints that exist in your auric field. This allows you to function as an objective observer. This, in turn, allows you to gather less subjective, more accurate information.

Do I still have free will? You learn to align your will with the will of your Oversoul and God-Mind. You begin to function as a funnel of energy. You are at the bottom, being constantly filled by your Oversoul and God-Mind. Rather than keep this energy, you constantly recycle it back up to your Oversoul.

You will learn that everything works like a fine-tuned machine when you recognize your constant state of communication with your Oversoul and God-Mind. You can still do whatever you want, but you will find out that when you listen to your Oversoul, life flows much easier for you.

Can a novice do it? You are already connected. Simply become aware that you are already connected. "Novice" is a term designed to complicate something that is simple. Just do it! Release the need to complicate.

Can I still have my spirit guides and helpers? Go to your Oversoul, and ask your Oversoul to explain who and what your "spirit guides and helpers" are. They may or may not be legitimate and/or helpful. They may simply be a product of your own mind-pattern. Only your Oversoul knows for sure. Go to the highest source available to you, then looking down, gather your explanations.

Can I still use crystals and stones? You can do whatever you want. Ask your Oversoul for explanation. Have it contact the Oversoul of the crystals and stones, and bring that information back to you. Find out your own information.

What about automatic writing and channeling? Automatic writing and channeling from your own Oversoul is one thing. But other than that, why would you want to allow any being or entity to possess your body? Each time an entity goes in or out, it is a tremendous shock, as well as destructive to the physical body. If you are only "listening" then writing or repeating, realize that you do not truly know the origins of these entities, or their goals. A con artist not in body is as dangerous as one in body. Access your own source. Stop looking for outer answers that will never be as accurate as your own inner answers. Spend your resources wisely.

Can I access information about other lifetimes? Absolutely. But, again, spend your resources wisely. Only do so if this serves a purpose. Curiosity is an expression of ego. Who cares if you are Queen Elizabeth in another lifetime unless it serves a purpose? And, if so, how does it directly affect your life experiences now?

Can I contact other dimensions, species, and/or even the departed through my Oversoul? Absolutely. But, again, spend your resources wisely. You can be led on a horizontal chase on any level that you attain. Focus your mind-pattern on vertical growth. Go as deeply and quickly into your source as you can. Whatever you choose to study, do so with awareness. Release your need for game playing and entertainment. Accomplish your goals. Time is of the essence.

Are there other people in my Oversoul? There are many soul-personalities experiencing God-Mind through your Oversoul, some in this dimension, some not. Each individual is important to its Oversoul. Each individual consists of unique experiences that contribute to the whole. As an analogy, think of the cells and organs in your body. Each cell and organ has a specific role and function. Your heart contributes something that your liver does not, and vice versa. Your body does not need two hearts or two livers. In the same way, each individual that belongs to the same Oversoul contributes his/her own unique experiences in his/her exploration of God-Mind.

How do I recognize other people in my Oversoul? First of all, they feel like they are a part of you. This feeling is something that you do not have to question or doubt. It is like finding an arm or a leg – you do not have to question whether it is yours or not. Secondly, they will not be "exactly like you" because one Oversoul would never have two soul-personalities going through the same experiences. Every soul-personality will be complementary to the other, but not duplicate another.

Do animals have Oversouls? Everything has an Oversoul for effective communication with God-Mind. Sometimes these are referred to as a "group-mind." There are many Oversouls within the mineral kingdom, the plant kingdom, the animal kingdom, and within each species. This forms an efficient hierarchy of communication all the way up to God-Mind.

Where can I find more detailed information about Oversoul communication? The best place is inside of yourself. You can also read my *In Search of Yourself* series. They all revolve around Oversoul communication. If you must choose only one, choose Book 1, *The Beginning*. The books are simply written. No matter where you are on your course of study, you are never beyond the basics.

*"In True Reality there is only One Soul.
This One Soul can never separate from Itself."*

God~Mind Experiencing Itself

Physical realities are the natural Self-Compartmentalizations of God-Mind exploring Itself. In True Reality, God-Mind can never separate from Itself, only create this illusion for the purpose of exploring Its own totality. Physical realities provide a vehicle for this Grand Internal Dissection.

Every species of plant, animal, mineral, and physical being that exists is a compartmentalization/subpersonality of God-Mind. A part of God-Mind becomes the species to understand and know Itself through experiential exploration. Every individual within the species is a cell within God-Mind, each one unique with at least one differentiating characteristic from all others. God-Mind "isolates" Itself, cell by cell, for Self-Exploration. In this way, each subpersonality within God-Mind continually explores and defines Itself.

For example, there are 20,000 known species of butterflies alone. Within each of these 20,000 known species, there is every variation that can possibly be imagined. This species is really a compartmentalization of God-Mind, twisting and turning on a Self-Exploratory journey.

Physical beings are merely another compartmentalization/ subpersonality of God-Mind.Every type of physical being that you can imagine exists somewhere, someplace. In Its quest for Internal Knowledge, physical beings are continually compartmentalized into more subpersonalities of God-Mind so that It can continue Its Self-Exploration.

On the soul-personality level, this compartmentalization is enhanced via the illusion of separation. As a cell within a subpersonality of God-Mind, the individual stays focused in its own compartment via this illusion. Within this illusion, the soul-personality asks the following questions: What is separation from God-Mind? From my Oversoul? From my parents? From my family? From myself? From a physical body? From others? How many ways can I separate from others? How many ways can I separate from myself? How many ways can others separate me from myself?

Keeping this in mind, understand that group or individual mind-control is a continuation of the compartmentalization process. Mind-control is another way that the illusion of separation is perpetuated so that compartmentalization can occur. When you think that you cannot compartmentalize/sepa-rate anymore, you find out that you can. The sub-personality of God-Mind must explore Its ability to compartmentalize until It cannot compartmentalize any more. Every cell must compartmentalize until there are no more ways left to compartmentalize. Only then can Its exploration be complete. Consider the following simplified model:

God-Mind compartmentalizes into Oversouls

Oversouls compartmentalize into soul-personalities

Soul-personalities compartmentalize into subpersonalities/alters

Subpersonalities/alters compartmentalize ad infinitum

Each compartmentalization perpetuates the illusion that it is separate from the whole. These compartmentalizations allow all aspects of God-Mind to continually experience Itself via the illusion of separation. In this artificially created scenario, the soul-personality becomes angry and despondent as it seemingly wanders further and further away from its Source. It is so fully immersed in the illusion that it looks to find its way "back" to God-Mind.

When the soul-personality is compartmentalized as much as it deems necessary, either by self or others, then it is time to create another illusion—that of "unification." The reverse process happens. As each piece "reintegrates," each cell brings its own unique set of knowledge to add to the whole. Now, the "pieces come together" and the whole understands the totality of Itself through unification. Consider the following simplified model:

Subpersonalities/alters unify with other subpersonalities/alters

Alters unify with main soul-personality

Soul-personality unifies with Oversoul

Oversoul unifies with God-Mind

This is the natural rhythm of the Universe, or the Breath of God-Mind. As God-Mind breathes Itself out, the soul-personality feels itself moving "away" from God-Mind. As God-Mind breathes Itself in, the soul-personality rides the breath "back" to its Source. As a microcosm of the macrocosm, the physical body replicates this breathing in and out.

Compartmentalization occurs on the Out-Breath. Unification occurs on the In-Breath. Both answer the same question from a different perspective. Together, they are the answer. In True Reality there is only One Soul. This One Soul can never separate from Itself. Compartmentalization via the illusion of separation is the best that It can do. Unification is only an illusion as well, as God-Mind can never separate from Itself in True Reality.

Have you ever heard someone say that he/she is "only a novice" or a "beginner" when it comes to metaphysics? Or, "I wish I could communicate with my Oversoul and/or God-Mind?" These people are definitely "into" the illusion of separation! ***There are no novices or beginners!*** Everyone *is* in communication with his/her Oversoul and God-Mind! ***There is no separation!*** Only illusion that allows the continual, fascinating process of Self-Exploration.

"Lifelong feelings of depression and suicide are often the result of programming abuse."

Are You Specifically Programmed?

Many people are wondering if they are specific targets of mind-control and programming. Because every effort is made to erase memory of this from the conscious mind, it is difficult for most people to reconcile their current life with the possibilities of a "secret life." There are some clues that you can use to begin to make this determination. Having one or more of these clues may or may not indicate specific mind-control and programming.

Most people who are specifically targeted for mind-control have the genetics that support this. People with blond or red hair, as well as blue or green eyes are the most programmable and easily controllable. People with a high degree of "psi" abilities in their families are desirable. People related to Illuminati family bloodlines, no matter how distant, are desirable. Dark-skinned people are less controllable and therefore less likely to be targeted. However, programming of these people does exist, especially on those who are needed to fulfill specific goals and missions.

Lifelong feelings of depression and suicide are often the result of programming abuse. The "princess and the pea" story is a good allegory. In the story, no matter how many mattresses the princess piles up, she can still feel the pea beneath them all. Programming abuse may be the "pea" that always causes discomfort no matter what you do. "Masked memories" may have you thinking that your family or friends were the perpetrators of the abuse. You might want to look beyond this.

Programmers believe that programming is carried in the genetic memory so that each generation within a family is increasingly more programmable. The same methods are often used in families, i.e., "successful" methods used on one family member will most likely be tried on another. If anyone in your family, or extended family, is a mind-control target, there is a high probability that you are as well.

Programmed people generally do not like such things as flashing or bright lights, high-pitched sounds, and rotating fans. These are all reminiscent of the programming experience. While many do not care for doctors, dentists are even a far greater fear—the chair, bright lights, and the feeling of loss of control can be overwhelming.

Those who feel that they have no control often try the hardest to exert control over others, food, exercise, and/or environment. Because they feel such a lack of control they are determined to create an area of their life over which they definitely have control. This can lead to an almost obsessive compulsive behavior of control issues.

Obsessive compulsive behavior is often a sign of mind-control and programming, including anorexia and bulimia. Anything that is repetitive continually re-emphasizes programming. The desire to self-inflict pain may be a sign.

If you have any strange body markings, or markings that suddenly appear, make note of these, including sores that do not heal. Use castor oil on them, and flush with violet to clean and deactivate. Nighttime vomiting, night sweats, nightmares and night terrors, are possible reactions to programming. Conversely, programmed people are programmed not to dream so that information planted deep within the matrix has less chance of surfacing into the conscious mind. So, not remembering dreams at all may be a sign of programming. Or, if you have consistent dreams of going up and/or down elevators, escalators, ladders, slides, etc., this could be indicative of going to different alters.

Buzzing, humming, or high-pitched noises while sleeping, especially in the early morning hours, are all attempts to push you out of your body. Out of body experiences, hearing voices, "channeling," and/or experiencing bone-chilling cold from which you cannot get warm may be symptoms of mind-control. Feeling pressure around your forehead or over the top of your head may be symptoms.

Classic "alien" abduction scenarios, including missing time, are often used as "masked memories" to cover up mind-control and programming. Feelings that you are "special" separate you from others. Feeling isolated and lonely are often the result, combined with the reinforcement "not to tell" because no one will understand. The ability to easily disassociate when life becomes comfortable may be a sign.

Because most programming is done by males via the root chakra, there are a large variety of sexual issues that happen as a result, ranging from total sexual dysfunction to promiscuity. Sexual identity issues may be prevalent in programmed males. Most pedophiliacs were sexually abused, thus inappropriately acting out what happened to them. Now they are the ones "in control." This can be the result of programming.

Extreme behaviors are often the result of the programming that pushes the target to extremes to achieve the desired results. Targets may overuse drugs and alcohol, which are often used in programming, or they may completely avoid them. Targets may never quite complete their goals, or they may try to reach their goal with an almost desperation. They may have an inability to enjoy any accomplished goals.

Irrational fears, panic attacks, paranoia, the inability to focus and/ or concentrate, sudden behavior changes, aggressive or violent outbursts, or even the inability to function at all may be symptoms of programming and mind-control. Some targets exhibit post-traumatic syndrome symptoms.

The colors that you use or are drawn to may be indicative of programming, especially bright yellow, bright red, black, white, and dark green. Sometimes, other people may tell you that you have a "Satanic" feel when you feel completely the opposite about yourself.

Most programmed people are highly intelligent. They function like "normal," every day people in most areas of their life. Their intelligence tells them that something is not right, but they cannot figure out what that is.

These are some of the more prevalent clues of programming. They may or may not be symptoms of programming. As you read the list, you need to look at your overall life to determine if this applies to you. Perhaps with some of this information, previously unexplainable circumstances may now make more sense. Take everything a step at a time. If you realize that you are programmed, the information is really not new to you—only new to the conscious mind now operating the "system."

"Once you are 'triggered,' anything can happen depending upon your specific programming."

What Is A Trigger?

Everyone has triggers for something. Perhaps when you walk past a bakery, the pleasant smells remind you of wonderful times at your grandparents' home. The smell "triggers" a memory. A specific song playing on the radio may remind you of a specific day, time, or event. If someone angrily yells that "you don't know what you are doing," you may be triggered into feeling and reacting like a two year old when your parents used to scold you. You may see a picture that will automatically trigger an internal reaction. Going to a certain place may trigger a buried memory. Similarly, one event may remind you of yet something else.

Triggers can be smells, words, sounds, pictures, places, events, or a combination of these. Triggers may be pleasant or unpleasant; positive or negative. You may or may not consciously know what triggers you. For example, consciously, you may not think about your grandparents when you inhale the bakery smells. You may just feel pleasant without specifically labeling, or even knowing, why. Consciously, you may not remember being two when your parents used to scold you. But, your habit response to these words always generates a specific reaction no matter who says them. You may not consciously remember why you do or do not like a specific song. You may just react to it one way or the other.

These "triggers" happen every day. Most people do not know themselves well enough to understand if they are reacting only to the present moment, or if they are reacting to the "moment before the moment," i.e., reacting to the past, using the present to trigger a past reaction.

These automatic reactions are really habit responses. A habit response is an established pattern of behavior that allows you to react to any given situation without thinking. For example, if someone waves, most people automatically wave back. If someone hands something to you, most people automatically reach out to take it. In the same way, you automatically respond to the triggers, as described above, without thinking. Only you know your personal triggers.

These triggers as mentioned above are internal triggers created by you without any outside help. You created them all yourself. People who have been specifically programmed have triggers that were externally installed within them. Because of the methods used to create these triggers, specifically programmed people are often triggered by a greater variety of external stimuli that remind them of the actual programming process.

In addition to the triggers already listed, these may include such things as high-pitched noises, flashing or bright lights, rotating fans, and even being in a dentist or doctor's chair (feeling a loss of control). Because most programming involves opening the person through the root chakra, sexual experiences are often triggers.

Neurolinguistic programming is a direct result of mind-control/ programming techniques. You see/hear/smell/touch/taste one thing (trigger) and you do something else. For example, when you see your set of keys (trigger) you remember to take a magazine to give to a friend. Specifically programmed people may be purposefully given or shown a word, sound, picture, etc. that unlocks something programmed in since childhood. The extent of the programming shows forth in the person's automatic reaction to the trigger.

Once you are "triggered," anything can happen depending upon your specific programming. You may become hard-hearted and virtually emotionless. You may withdraw, disassociate, become distant, and/or robotic-like, feeling like you are going through the motions without exactly knowing why but unable to stop, or even without wanting to stop.

You may go to the other extreme and become wildly emotional, seemingly without any control, and again, without any desire to stop. You may think of doing something that you would not ordinarily do. If you are able to pull yourself together (literally) enough, to try to stop your behavior you may become extremely depressed and suicidal. These are reactions to internal programs that tell you if you do not carry out your programs you are to self-destruct. Most specifically programmed people have self-destruct programs of some type. The trigger may even bring forth an alter that may do things that the conscious part of you would not.

When you respond to a trigger, you are said to be "activated." How long you stay in this activated state varies according to the individual. If you feel yourself become activated by a trigger, mentally create the brown merger archetype on a royal blue background at the pineal gland immediately. If you cannot do this, contact someone that you trust for help. He/she can mentally do this for you, and can even draw this on paper for you to look at or keep upon your person. Also use the violet bubble with a mirror around it and/or the ultraprotection technique to prevent ELF transmissions from entering your auric field.

This is why it is so important to know yourself. Determine your internally created triggers as well as any that may have been externally placed into you. Clean them all out by releasing everything up to your Oversoul as you find them, incorporating the brown merger archetype at the pineal gland into the exercise when you find external controls. However you do it, take control of yourself so that no one and no thing has control over you.

The public collective consciousness can also be triggered into a group reaction. For example, when people's children are being gunned down at school, the automatic response is "take away everyone's guns." When people are collectively programmed to believe that Moslems are a global threat, the collective consciousness automatically responds accordingly. The collective's emotions can be turned on and turned off, and directed so that people believe the solution came from within.

Whether you are programmed as a member of the general populace, whether you have been specifically targeted, or whether you "programmed" yourself, you have triggers. Only you have the power to find and diffuse them. Time is of the essence, as emphasized by our rapidly changing times.

"The programmers know who and what you are before you are born."

Self~Deprogramming

Programmers only use what already exists within you. This includes personality traits and simultaneous lifelines. Programmers use inherent basics to mold the target into whatever meets their particular needs. They take what already exists, subverting it before you can discover and utilize its full potential. These parts of yourself were basically programmed to be used against you. You can reclaim/reintegrate these parts plus use this extra "training" to advance self-knowledge. What was used against you can now be used "for" you. By understanding your programming, you find keys to who and what you already are.

The programmers know who and what you are before you are born. They recognize the soul-personality and read its frequency. They create a specific body using specific genetics for a specific soul-personality. Often, they bring people together for breeding purposes only so that specific genetics and/or lineages are mixed for their specific reasons. Parents' of programmed people often tell the same story—they were going to marry one person, but they suddenly found themselves marrying someone else. They marry for reasons other than love—money, convenience, sometimes they admit that they do not even know why they got married in the first place—it just happened.

This is one reason for the high divorce rate. After the children are created, then the parents are specifically broken apart. A home that is not stable creates a less stable child that is more easily controllable. Once the body is genetically created, the programmers sometimes place a "captured" soul-personality into the body. Or, they know the type of soul-personality that will be attracted into a specific body and they wait for it to arrive. Either way, they know the intricacies of the soul-personality before the soul-personality knows itself.

Programming is often started before birth or shortly thereafter, depending upon the plan for the soul-personality. Because of this, the process of programming is so integral to the soul-personality that consciously it does not recognize that any tampering has occurred. In fact, the "abnormal" is so normal to the developing conscious part of the soul-personality, that it most likely does not even stop to question these abnormalities.

For example, getting up in the night to vomit may be "normal" to the conscious mind if this is all that he/she has known. Even being taken, nocturnal visits, or seeing things that most people do not. Because this is customary and all the child has ever consciously known, he/she does not ever think to question this. The child may never bring it up to the parents. If it is spoken about, the parents may not recognize what is happening or merely think that the child has an overactive imagination.

Programmers install a matrix that acts as a map to the overall "system." This is how the programmer (most often male) finds his way around the soul-personality. Every person's matrix is ultimately unique to him/her because it is based upon a unique soul-personality. However, the programmer may prefer specific programs for specific soul-personalities, or may use similar methods of "installation" (torture) on many different subjects.

There may be many different major programs installed within one system. There may be Wizard of Oz programming, End Time programming, Alice in Wonderland programming, etc. within one system. There may be alters that are adolescents, remain at the ages of two or three, ones that spy on other alters or people, sexual slaves, etc. Each program and alter has its intricacies, and each one serves a specific purpose. There may be dozens or hundreds of each within every system.

Programming matrixes are cubes of 13 compartments by 13 compartments by 13 compartments. Within each of the 2197 total compartments there is a program or a part of a program. The 13x13x13 cube is chosen because this is the same holographic matrix upon which this physical reality is built. Many programmed people report seeing a cube or some type of matrix.

Because of the complexity of the artificially installed system, it is imperative that you take notes. As you record the "abnormal" events in your life, you will begin to realize that what you once considered normal may also be abnormal, as previously discussed. The bits and pieces of information are the keys to helping you put your story together. Pay attention to the subconscious clues that are all around you. For example, what kind of "doodles" do you create when idly drawing to pass the time? Spirals that indicate movement into other realities? Daisies from the "I love you, I love you not" program? Satanic five-pointed stars? Hour glasses to indicate time passing with consequences? Do you have messages trying to get through from your subconscious mind via your dream state?

What are your idiosyncrasies? What strange little habits do you have and where do they come from? The more you record, the more that you will begin to realize what may have been artificially enhanced.

The brown merger archetype is a primary one used in self-deprogramming. It tells all parts of self to merge together.

This is the opposite of any artificially installed compartmentalization. If you suspect that you are specifically programmed, keep this archetype at the pineal gland at all times. Keeping the brown merger archetype at the pineal gland, place your memories, thoughts, and questions on top of it. With your eyes closed, concentrate and focus. Make notes of what comes up. If you feel traumatized at any time, ground yourself in brown and bring yourself out of it. Use the following affirmation:

I am 100% internally controlled by Self, Oversoul, and God-Mind.

My mind-pattern is impenetrable.

My mind-pattern is invincible.

You can also visualize the 13x13x13 cube with its 2197 compartments. In each compartment place a brown merger archetype. Then flush the entire matrix in violet. See the brown merger archetypes merging into one at the pineal gland, as the matrix behind it crumbles. Finally, bring the final merger symbol from the cube into the merger symbol already at your pineal gland. Take the process a step at a time. While your tendency might be to rush forward, recognize that the artificial installations were intended to permanently exist within you. There are many built-in pitfalls to stop you from undoing your programming. Keep this in mind as you slowly unravel and merge your programming.

Deprogramming takes time and must be done slowly. When people suspect, or know, that they are specifically programmed, most become overanxious to complete the process. When you realize that you might possibly be able to gain answers to questions that have plagued you for a lifetime, you may think that you do not consciously have the patience to slowly move through the process. Most people want their answers "yesterday."

Most likely, this will not happen as quickly as you would like. During programming, the brain itself is "rewired" so that the soul-personality is limited in its ability to function through the brain. In addition, there are often implants that enhance the programmer's work. These may be organic or partially organic, meaning that they are an integral part of the system. It is not so simple to just remove them, so it is best to work on deactivating them through use of a violet flush. And, as the holes in your mind-pattern are mended and it no longer accepts such invasive technology, it is possible to permanently release these from the physical body.

Through the process of deprogramming, you will begin to find your "triggers," or what specifically may have a tendency to activate you. When these triggers come up when you are in control, flush them with violet and merge them into the system. The idea is to have control of them so that they do not control you when your guard is down. The more conscious that you can become of your externally installed programming and what triggers it, the more control you can have over it.

You can become triggered and activated during deprogramming. It is also possible for you to go into an alter, and not be able to stop any of it. This is simply a reaction to a very sophisticated network that has been artificially installed within you. For what you have been through, this is a natural reaction.

For these reasons it is important to go slowly, integrating each step along the way. It is necessary to be consistent and persistent. If you have someone with whom you can discuss your situation, this is even better. This person can help to ground you and may be able to pull you out of it should your triggers become activated, and/or you go into an alter.

If someone that you know becomes activated, then it is especially important that you emotionally tie into his/her heart chakra, with permission on the Oversoul level. Isolation is part

125

of the programming process, and this includes emotional as well as physical isolation. For this reason, you must work on the inner levels to reduce the emotional isolation. Words are meaningless, so do your inner level work.

When a person becomes activated and/or goes into an alter, he/she can go one of two ways. First, he/she may become entirely irrational with wild emotions, or he/she may become totally void of all emotions. If this should happen, put the person in brown to ground him/her. Spin the chakras, keep the T-Bar balanced, and speak to him/her on the Oversoul level. Use a violet cord from your heart to his/hers. "Plump" up the heart area, which most likely has been energetically/emotionally shriveled, with medium green as well as pale pink for unconditional love. This will help put him/her back into his/her feeling nature, replacing the isolated, detached state into which an alter moves.

Successful deprogramming is a two-edged sword, especially as you work through the programs that have been installed and into the methods of installation which usually involve torture, sexual abuse, and possibly murderous acts and blood rituals.

As you move through your current programs, you will also encounter the actual programming that occurred as a child. This creates an entirely new set of issues, including parental abandonment (why did my parents let this happen to me?) and such thoughts as: Why did I allow this to happen in the first place? What is my inherent personality that invited this in? Was I involved in programming/controlling/handling in other simultaneous lifelines?

Most programmed people have suicide programs within them. When you get close to uncovering a truth, or disabling an active program, the suicide programs kick in. The positive side is that you are getting close to the truth. The negative side is that there may be a part of you that does not want to live to discover that truth.

Again, do your chakra spinning, T-Bar balancing, flush with violet, work on your heart chakra, take sea salt baths to help negate the effects of ELF, and/or talk to someone that you can trust. Be mindful of the colors that you choose to wear so that you are not enhancing any ELF that you may be picking up, i.e., avoid bright yellow, bright red, black, white, and dark green. Simply becoming aware of what is happening is the first part in taking back your control. Recognize that if you give into these urges, then "they" win. Do not let them win—let this thought be your motivation for living, if it comes to that.

As you begin to recognize your triggers, you can begin to avoid them. When you face them without a reaction, you will know that you are making progress. Sometimes you may need to take a break from the deprogramming process. As you deprogram, you may re-experience the same things that happened during the programming process—headaches, vomiting, flashing/flickering light sensitivity, "unsettled" feelings, etc. If this happens, put yourself in brown, give yourself a rest from the process, and when you are feeling better, start with your work again.

While it is important to go slowly, it is important to move steadily through your programming, especially for people who have "time-sensitive" programming. Sometimes there are programs that are built into specific events or dates. Again, if you can deprogram yourself before these events or dates happen, then you will not be vulnerable to acting out your programming.

It is possible to discover your triggers without becoming activated by them, but this takes a willingness to slowly but methodically move through the programming. As always, use what you know, keep your journals, and use your affirmations. Deprogramming leads you into the dark side of yourself, which only means that you are exploring another part of God-Mind Itself.

www.stewartswerdlow.com

Visit the *Expansions* website to read the latest up-to-date information on:

Daily Practical Tips
Current Event & News Postings
Stewart's Column: *Stewart Says...*
Janet's Articles: *Belief Systems Shattered*
Janet's Column: *Dear Friends*
Dream Center
Life Support Group™ and Leader Contacts
Latest Books, Videos, & Products
Seminars, Lectures, & Events
Contributing Authors....and Much More!